What Would Dad Say?

Now that He's in Heaven

David Nelms and Bill Yeargin

Copyright © 2020, David Nelms and Bill Yeargin

All rights reserved. No part of this book may be used or reproduced by any means, graphic, electronic, or mechanical (including any information storage retrieval system) without the express written permission from the author, except in the case of brief quotations for use in articles and reviews wherein appropriate attribution of the source is made.

Originally published by
Brentwood Christian Press
4000 Beallwood Avenue
Columbus, GA 31904

Republished by
Ignite Press
5070 N 6th St. #189
Fresno, CA 93710
www.IgnitePress.us

ISBN: 978-1-950710-80-5 (Amazon Print)
ISBN: 978-1-950710-81-2 (IngramSpark) PAPERBACK
ISBN: 978-1-950710-82-9 (Smashwords)

You may contact the author at:

billyeargin@gmail.com

Because of the dynamic nature of the Internet, web addresses or links contained in this book may have been changed since publication and may no longer be valid. The content of this book and all expressed opinions are those of the author and do not reflect the publisher or the publishing team. The author is solely responsible for all content included herein.

Dedication

To our moms:

We know how important each of you was to our fathers. We also know that without you, our fathers couldn't have been the men they were. We love you very much.

To our families:

David's--Loretta, Charity, Jared, and Jesse. Bill's--Leigh, Erin, and Amanda.

If we have learned anything in writing this book, it is that we should continually strive to be better husbands and fathers. Luckily, we had good examples set for us in our fathers. We love you very much.

Table of Contents

A Word from Bill 1

A Word from David 4

Chapter 1: What Would Dad Say About Sickness? 7

Chapter 2: What Would Dad Say About Death? 11

Chapter 3: What Would Dad Say About Heaven? 15

Chapter 4: What Would Dad Say About Mom? 23

Chapter 5: What Would Dad Say About Family? 27

Chapter 6: What Would Dad Say About Kids? 35

Chapter 7: What Would Dad Say About People? 43

Chapter 8: What Would Dad Say About Fear? 49

Chapter 9: What Would Dad Say About Grace? 59

Chapter 10: What Would Dad Say About Choices? 65

Chapter 11: What Would Dad Say About Right And Wrong? 69

Chapter 12: What Would Dad Say About Foundations? 75

Chapter 13: What Would Dad Say About Mental Health? 81

Chapter 14: What Would Dad Say About Tough Times? ... 87

Chapter 15: What Would Dad Say About Faith? 93

Chapter 16: What Would Dad Say About Time? 97

Chapter 17: What Would Dad Say About Money? 101

Chapter 18: What Would Dad Say About Science? 107

Chapter 19: What Would Dad Say About Church Traditions? 111

Chapter 20: What Would Dad Say About Life? 115

Conclusion: 121

About Our Dads 124

A Word from Bill

On February 10, 2001, I traveled from my home in Florida to Raleigh, North Carolina, as part of a business trip. On that cold, windy Saturday, I set out on a personal mission. Business was the last thing on my mind.

I rented a car at the Raleigh airport and drove north one hour to the little town of Oxford. That's where my dad is buried. For a combination of reasons, this was the first time since Dad died nearly three years ago that I had made this pilgrimage. I felt guilty for not having come sooner.

As I approached Oxford, memories flooded my mind. The sight of rolling hills and red clay took me back to a pleasant childhood. I rolled down my windows and breathed in the distinctive aroma of North Carolina pine trees. My grandparents had lived in Oxford their entire lives. Dad loved this city, too, and I spent a lot of time with him here.

Even the road signs triggered unique memories. My eyes stung as I tried to focus on the road ahead of me. I turned down Industry Drive, then onto Cherry Street. As I pulled into the cemetery, tears spilled onto my cheek.

I pulled up to Dad's gravesite, then just sat in the car, unable to move. I could not bear to look at the place where my father was buried. I focused on the grass, the trees, the flowers, anything but Dad's marker. Staring straight ahead, I brushed my damp face with the back of my hand. Finally I worked up the courage to look at Dad's grave. Fresh tears flowed down my cheeks.

I got out of the car and walked to the gravesite. I knew Dad's spirit was not there, but the body that used to hold me and protect me and play with me was buried there in the ground. It broke my heart to be so close to the body Dad had lived in.

As I stood by the grave, shivering against the cold wind, I reflected on many things, but one recurring thought overshadowed the rest. I couldn't get it out of my mind.

"What would Dad say to me if we could spend one more hour together right now?"

I thought about numerous topics and wondered what Dad's advice might be on each one, now that he had the perspective of eternity.

The hour I had allotted to spend at the cemetery flew by. I knew I had to leave so I could catch my next flight. But I didn't want to. Dad's gravesite now drew me like a magnet. I felt it would be disloyal of me to leave him there, but knew I must go.

As I drove back to Raleigh, I was obsessed by the question of what pad would say to me if we could have that hour together. I continued to sift through subjects in my mind, realizing that in many cases Dad's perspective would be far different from mine. Viewing life through the lens of eternity gave me a broader focus than I had ever had before.

Back home in Florida, I called my friend and pastor, David

Nelms. I told David about my experience at the cemetery in Oxford and how it was affecting my view of life.

David's father had also passed away, and he agreed that thinking about what our fathers' perspectives might be was a powerful, life-changing exercise. In business, it's called "seeing the big picture." This was the ultimate application of that concept.

Since David is a pastor, I trust his judgment on the eternal perspective a lot more than I do my own. But despite our different life experiences, we both believe there is a tremendous amount to be learned from taking an eternal perspective on life.

I hope reading this book will help you as much as writing it helped me.

Bill Yeargin

A Word from David

When Bill first asked me to assist in this book, my immediate response was, "I'm not qualified for such a feat. Find someone else!" But the more I thought about the subject of this book, the more interested I became.

I was blessed with what I consider to be the world's all-time greatest dad. I never heard him say a single word of profanity. I never knew him to tell a dirty joke, or even laugh at one. He never screamed at my mother. Dad was not perfect, but he was a lot closer to it than anyone I've ever known. My father was my hero. He was the best man at my wedding. He was my spiritual example. There was nothing he wouldn't do for me, and nothing I wouldn't do for him. During the final years of my dad's life, I pastored in Iowa and Dad lived in Georgia, so I was unable to spend a lot of time with him. I did, however, cherish our weekly phone calls, looking forward to them for days. We'd talk about nothing, and yet about everything. We discussed our family, the weather, and the Atlanta Braves. (He always said, "Go, Falcons! And take the Braves with you!")

When Dad got brain cancer, I wanted desperately to move back home to Georgia so I could be with him. I sensed his time on earth was short. I wanted to see him more than just one or two times a year.

But whenever I brought up the possibility to Dad, he always replied firmly, "Son, God led you to Iowa. Don't you dare move for me. We'll have all of eternity to be together."

I listened to my dad's council.

Dad reminded me often of the promise he had made to my mother early in their marriage, that if he died first, he would be waiting for her at heaven's Eastern Gate. As a family, we had all agreed to this heavenly arrangement.

One cold night in February, Mom called while my family was having dinner. When I heard her voice, I lost my appetite immediately. "David," she whispered, "your dad's gone. We'll meet him at the Eastern Gate."

After that call, I raced to my bedroom, locked the door, and turned off the light. I fell on my bed and wept until I had no more tears. The only words that came to my mind were those of Job, who cried out centuries ago at the graves of his ten children, "The Lord gives and the Lord takes away. Blessed be the name of the Lord." (Job 1:21)

Since his death, I have occasionally felt grief, remorse, and even guilt over not having been with my father during those final years. But I know he was right. As important as family is, there are some things that are even more important. Obeying God is one of them.

It's been six years since my father died. I still miss him dearly. I suppose I always will, until the day I see him again at heaven's Eastern Gate!

After Bill told me about his experience at his father's gravesite, I became consumed with the question, "What would my dad say to me today, from his heavenly perspective? Would his council be different from what it was while he was on this earth?"

Like Bill, the more I meditated on this, the more it changed me. It has helped me become a better man, hus-band, dad, pastor, and person. It is my sincere prayer it will do the same for you.

One final thought: Since Bill and I cannot literally speak to our dads, this book is obviously, to some degree, speculation. Perhaps when we approach them at the Eastern Gate, they'll be standing there shaking their heads, saying, "You guys got it all wrong. Where did you come up with all that stuff anyway?"

Maybe. Maybe not. I am convinced we're at least "in the ballpark."

St. Paul wrote, "Set your affections on things above, not on things of this earth" (Colossians 3:2, KJV). I believe I can hear both of our fathers saying, "Amen!"

David Nelms

Chapter 1

What Would Dad Say About Sickness?

*There are people who will spend eternity
in heaven with me because of my sickness!*

Dear Son,

I know how hard my illness was on our family, especially your mother. I saw your tears as my disease grew worse and you saw death drawing nearer every day.

I appreciate your sorrow for my suffering. It's perfectly normal to feel that way.

But all of that is over now. The negative aspects of my sickness mean nothing to me any longer. The pain I went through is as insignificant as a nanosecond in the light of eternity.

I am certainly full of vim and vigor now! In fact, I am happier and healthier than it is possible for you to imagine in your earthly mind.

Now that I'm here in heaven, I can see God's master plan for my life with perfect clarity. I realize that He had everything--even my sickness--under control. He knew exactly what He was doing.

All my life, I wanted God to use me for His glory. And He did! I'm glad He used my sickness to glorify Himself. I would happily do it all again, now that I see what God accomplished through it.

Many wonderful things came out of my illness. Those who were close to me at the time grew closer to God. People's lives were touched as they prayed for my recovery and spent more time in God's Word. Families were changed by watching our family bond during my final days on earth.

Best of all, there are people who will spend eternity in heaven with me *because of my sickness!*

Do you remember all those people your mom talked to about Christ during my stay in Hospice? Well, several of them have already accepted Christ! And one man, who was a Christian before he met us, was so blessed by our family's closeness that he stopped working late and started spending more time with his wife and kids.

Remember the lady whose unsaved husband was dying, and she and your mom were praying together everyday that he would accept Christ? He died just a few days before I passed. Well, guess what? He was right here waiting for me when I got to the Eastern gate! He gave me a great big hug and thanked me for my wife's prayers and her unfailing witness to him.

Son, you won't be able to completely understand this until you join me. But please don't let my suffering cause you to doubt God's wonderful grace. Don't let your memory of my illness become a weight that holds you back from doing what God wants you to do. My suffering must not become a barrier to your accomplishment of God's plan for your life.

You may not believe this, but I went through times of doubt myself. From the moment my disease was diagnosed, I questioned everything that was happening to me. That's a normal reaction. It's a lot easier to be upset and angry than it is to trust God. But in light of what I know today, I wish I had never doubted Him.

Even during the times when I questioned God, I knew deep in my soul that I could trust in His plan for me. I am praising Him today that I did.

God has been good to me! I love Him, and I'm grateful for the life, the illness, and the death He gave me. I wouldn't change a thing, even if I could.

I know feelings of sadness linger in your heart, Son, but it is important for you to move on. Don't let the devil weigh you down with doubts about God's grace. His plan is perfect, and someday you too will be amazed when you see how He used my sickness to glorify Him.

Too many people are tricked by the devil into wasting their time questioning God and worrying about things they cannot control. Don't be one of those people. Use every minute on earth that God has given you. Don't spend one moment questioning Him. Have faith in His plan. It's always perfect.

Finally, please forgive me for anything I said or did in my last days that may have hurt you, your mother, or any other members of our family. I was not myself during that time. The medication took over my mind so much I couldn't even think straight.

In addition, I realized that I was dying and would never see my grandkids graduate, get married, or have their own children. This really grieved me. If only I could have known that I would see them after all ... just from a different perspective.

I have a vague recollection of having said and done hurtful things to you and others as my body and brain became ravaged with disease. But thanks be to God, He has erased those scenes from my memory. Please, Son, let God erase them from yours as well. You must know that I didn't mean them. I wouldn't hurt you or your mother for anything in the world.

If you really want to respect my memory, Son, live your life planning for the day that we will be together again. That will be a glorious and happy time indeed!

I love you, Son.

Dad

Chapter 2

What Would Dad Say About Death?

For Christians, death is a sweet release
from suffering, pain, sorrow, and sadness.

Dear Son,

I know you sometimes feel angry about my death, that it just isn't fair that I'm gone. Life without me is more difficult for you and your family. You wonder what things would be like if I was still alive on earth. You grieve that your children, my grandchildren, no longer have my influence in their lives.

I understand completely how you feel, and of course I miss being with all of you. But death is a natural part of life. It is the one thing every living person has in common with each other.

Fear of death is perfectly normal. When I was alive, I was sometimes afraid of the process of dying, even though I never doubted where my spirit was going after my death. But let me tell you, there's nothing to fear! While the sickness that led to my death was excruciating, both physically and emotionally, death itself was not painful at all. It was a simple transition that instantly brought me here to my glorious new home.

I have seen your tears. I know your sadness. I understand

how much you miss my presence. But don't think for a moment that I am missing out on your life. On the contrary, I've been watching everything. And I have a panoramic view from up here!

I was there when you and your family had your first Thanksgiving without me. I know how difficult it was for you to take over the responsibility of carving the turkey, the job I cherished and looked forward to all year long.

Then, just a week or two later, I watched you shuffling through the stores trying to find Christmas presents for everybody. All you could see were things you thought would have made perfect gifts for me.

When you tried to celebrate that first Christmas Eve after I passed on, I appreciate that you held an empty seat in the pew in my memory. But it wasn't necessary. I was up here, but I was singing those Christmas carols right along with you, harmonizing beautifully with your wife and my granddaughters. (Yep, believe it or not, I've got the most gorgeous tenor voice you've ever heard--nothing like that gravely nasal noise I used to make!)

I saw you all go to bed early on New Year's Eve, even before Dick Clark's show started, because you couldn't bear to think of the coming year without me.

But, Son, you aren't without me! Just like Jesus, I'm still there, even though you can't see me. This new body of mine has the ability to skip around here in heaven and simultaneously watch the goings-on of my earthly family. How neat is that?

Remember that verse I often quoted during the last weeks

of my illness? The apostle Paul wrote in 2 Timothy 4:6, "My departure is at hand." That was the constant cry of my heart until the moment I left earth. Well, I was talking to Paul the other day, and he gave me some fascinating background on the word he used that we translate "departure."

It carries the idea of a boat pulling up anchor and sailing toward its point of origin, or an army breaking camp and marching home, or a slave being released from his chains. For the Christian, death is all of those things. It is a release from the prison of our failing bodies. It is the sailing away to heaven's golden shore. It is the breaking of camp and heading home. For Christians, death is a sweet release from suffering, pain, sorrow, and sadness.

When I died, I "departed" from earth. But at the same moment, I "arrived" in heaven. I was immediately transported directly into the presence of my Father God. It was like stepping out of a dark room into a world of glorious light.

I know how hard it was for you to speak at my funeral. But you have no idea how many lives were touched by the things you said. I am constantly running into people here whose friends and loved ones were in attendance that day.

I also know how uncomfortable you felt about the idea of videotaping my funeral. Thanks for giving in to your mother's request. Several of the people who received copies of that tape rededicated their lives to Christ after viewing it. One young man, who overheard his mother watching the tape in the next room, gave his life to Christ after hearing it. You will probably not meet him during the course of your life on earth, but I can't wait to introduce the two of you to each other after you both get here.

Death proves that life is uncertain. Never take anything for granted, not one second. Every morning, thank God for another day to live, and then enjoy it to the fullest.

Overcoming your pain and grief over my death is a test of your faith. It is an opportunity for you to prove out everything I taught you while I was living on earth. If you truly believe in heaven, and I know you do, you will be able to live as though I'm on an extended vacation in the most beautiful tropical paradise ever created. Although I won't be returning, you will one day meet me here. What a glorious day that will be!

When the time draws near for you to join me, do not allow Satan to steal your joy. During your last days, as you prepare yourself for "departure," rest assured that I will be eagerly awaiting your arrival.

See you soon!

I love you, Son.

Dad

Chapter 3

What Would Dad Say About Heaven?

Heaven is so incredible,
I can't imagine ever going back to earth.

Dear Son,

I know sometimes you find yourself feeling sorry for me because I left earth sooner than any of us expected. It saddens you to think about the things I missed out on--watching the grandkids grow up, attending their graduations, being there for their weddings and babies and other significant events.

The truth is, I haven't missed a thing! I continue to follow your lives. In fact, I've had a front-row seat the whole time. And you wouldn't believe the view--it's awesome!

Of course I miss you, your mother, and your children. But the truth is, I wouldn't leave this place if you paid me. (Not that money means anything up here, anyway!)

Do you remember the story in John 11 where Jesus raised Lazarus from the dead? Of course you do. I remember when you were in fifth grade, and your Sunday school teacher made you pick a Bible verse to memorize. You chose John 11:35 because it was the shortest. Just two words: "Jesus wept." But that little verse says so much about our Lord and Savior!

Have you ever wondered why Jesus cried just before He raised Lazarus from the dead? It wasn't because Lazarus had died. Jesus knew he wasn't going to stay dead. On the contrary, due to His great love for Lazarus, Jesus hated to make him leave heaven and return to the sorrows and pains of earth where, among other things, he would have to die all over again. (By the way, I've talked to Lazarus about that, and he tells me he put up quite a fuss when he found out he had to go back!)

Heaven is so incredible, I can't imagine ever going ba.ck to earth. This place is as good as it gets. It's perfect! And you can't improve on perfection.

Maybe if I try to describe my new home to you, it will be a comfort and encouragement to you and your mother. So here goes. I'll give it my best shot!

First of all, let me tell you what we *don't* have here:

- Cemeteries or funeral homes. No one dies up here.
- Hospitals, medical clinics, or pharmacies. Nobody here gets sick.
- Smokestacks polluting the air, or toxic waste sites polluting the seas. Everything here is pristine and uncontaminated.
- Bars on the windows or locks on the doors. Heaven's gates remain open perpetually.
- Prisons, jails, or police force. There's no Army, Air Force, Navy, or Marines. We don't even have a Coast Guard. Heaven is a place of perfect peace and safety.
- Starving or suffering children. You will not find a

single little one whose hair has fallen out due to chemotherapy. The word *cancer* is not in heaven's dictionary.
- Blind, death, or disabled people. There are no wheelchairs, nursing homes, rehab centers, or orphanages in my new home.
- Natural disasters, such as hurricanes, tornadoes, floods, earthquakes, fires, and famines. All of heaven is in absolute submission to His Majesty.
- Domestic disputes. No slugging it out in court.
- Darkness or shadows. In heaven, there's constant and continual light.
- Weariness. Do you remember all those naps I used to take in the late afternoons and evenings? I haven't had a nap since I walked through heaven's front door!
- Crime, divorce, abortion, cheating, hatred, or jealousy. Lying, lust, and laziness have no place in perfection. There's no bitterness, malice, or unfor- giveness, and no immorality of any kind.
- Discrimination, racial prejudice, ethnic cleansing, or war. Up here, there's only one race: the race of the redeemed ones. Everyone here lives in perfect harmony and unity.
- Denominational divisions. Son, did you know there are no Baptists in heaven? Neither are there any Presbyterians, Episcopalians, Methodists, Lutherans, or Catholics. We're all just Christians here.
- Best of all, there's no trace of sin or rebellion against

God.

Now I'd like to tell you about what we *do* have here. The truth is, it would take an eternity to describe this place accurately. You remember that song we used to sing in church--the one that says that even after we've been in heaven for ten thousand years, we'll have no less days to praise Him than when we started? I always thought that was an exaggeration. Boy, was I wrong!

Up here, you'll find:

- Perfect love, true peace (which really does pass all understanding), joy unspeakable, and grace without end.
- Beauty. Wait until you see the tree of life with its twelve different fruits. And the river of life! Until you've seen it, you can't truly understand the meaning of the word *sparkle*. And when you consider its source--the very throne of God--you understand why. I could tell you about the streets of gold, the walls of jasper, and the gates of pearl, but those things are practically overlooked up here.
- Wonderful animals. The animal kingdom is amazingly represented here. On my first day, I saw the most gorgeous, breathtaking creatures I'd ever seen: heaven's white horses. And hold on to your seat, Son. They can fly! I don't mean they run fast. They literally fly!
- Brilliant stars. Wait until you see them. What a sight to behold!

- Praise. All creation (outside of earth) honors its Creator. When He walks by, the trees of the field literally clap their hands for joy as their branches bow down in reverence before Him.
- Heaven's angels. God's fiery creatures of light are awesome in their strength and completely loyal to their Lord. They live to please Him. It matters not what He tells them to do. Their delight is in honor-ing Him.
- Music. Cherubim and seraphim, angelic creatures that hover in His presence, do nothing but chant, "Holy, holy, holy, Lord God Almighty, which was and is and is to come." Son, I've been here for years now, and they haven't stopped saying it yet. I'm told they'll still be at it when time ends and eternity begins. I never get tired of hearing them honor God. Wait until you hear them sing! You think your church choir is something. Here, the music is ... well, heavenly!
- People--from every corner of the globe. The stories of how they came to know Godwould bring tears to our eyes ... if we could cry! By the way, I've bumped into many people who have been touched by your ministry on earth. Don't be discouraged by the circumstances of life, Son. You *are* making a difference! An eternal difference.

Remember that old man in Maryland, the one who lived in that tiny, beat-up trailer and wheezed whenever he tried to speak? Remember how everyone called him an old drunk?

Well, he's not drunk now ... unless maybe drunk with joy!

He no longer wheezes when he speaks. As a matter of fact, he sings praises to the Lord with the best of them. And he has closets now that are bigger than his whole trailer!

Son, that old man was a heartbeat away from a terrible eternity when you found him and told him about Christ. I'm so glad you did!

He can't wait to see you and thank you personally for making an eternal difference in his life.

I could go on forever about the wonderful things we have in heaven ... literally! But the most important thing of all is that God is here. That's right! God the Almighty. The Creator Himself. My eyes have actually seen Him. My fingers have touched the nail prints in His hands. I've knelt on my face before His feet. His eyes of fire have gazed into my soul. I've experienced, first hand, His divine love for me.

And guess what else? He has given me a new name, just like He said He would in the book of Revelation. A nick-name just for me, given by God Himself, that only He and I know. What an honor!

Do you remember my favorite song on earth? I loved to sing about coming to the garden alone. Well, Son, I now experience that song every moment of every day. He truly walks with me and talks with me and tells me I am His own. And the joy we've shared is unique to us. No other person has ever known the special relationship my Savior and I share.

I'm telling you, Son, heaven is everything you ever dreamed it would be, and more.

Oh, yes, one last thing. I've also seen His book. You know, the Book of Life? And yes, Son, your name is written in it.

Your mansion is right down the street from mine. I can hardly wait to welcome you home.

I'll be waiting at the Eastern Gate to show you the way.

I love you, Son.

Dad

Chapter 4

What Would Dad Say About Mom?

*I charge you now with the responsibility and
the privilege of taking care of your mother.*

Dear Son,

The most important person in my life was your mother, my wife. You know how much I loved her when I was on earth. Let me tell you, I love her even more now. I was the most blessed man who ever lived because I was able to spend so many years with that amazing woman. God has truly poured out His blessings on our family through her. She is a godly wife, a nurturing mother, my best friend, the love of my life, and my eternal helpmate.

Your mother is a strong woman, stronger than people may think. Since I left earth, she has had to make many important decisions without me, and she's doing a wonderful job. Her life is built on the Rock, Jesus Christ. She is resting in His arms, now that mine are no longer there to hold her. I charge you now with the responsibility and the privilege of taking care of your mother. I know you're busy, but your mother's well-being must be one of your top priorities. Many adults get so wrapped up in their own lives that they forget about taking care of the one who raised them. I know you wouldn't be that selfish. But it's easy to get so distracted by day-to-day activities that you forget to think about your mother's needs and wants. Don't let that happen. Be mindful of your mother's security. Make sure she lives the rest of her life in a safe environment with which both of you are comfortable. Be diligent in seeking what is best for her, protect her from danger, and give her the gift of peace that comes from knowing you are looking out for her.

Your mother has been very lonely since my death. Even though that's perfectly natural, don't take her pain lightly. Visit her often. Call her even more often. Comfort her with your presence. Don't wait until her loneliness builds up to the point where it is more than she can bear.

Listen to your mother whenever she needs to talk. Be proactive in this area by asking her how she feels. Let her know you're truly interested in what she has to say. Tell her she can talk to you any time she needs to. Just knowing you are willing to listen will make her feel much better.

When she does have something to say, give her your undivided attention. Don't allow yourself to be so distracted by thoughts about your own concerns that you don't truly listen to her. Unlike us men, women often work through things by talking about them to someone else. They don't always want us to come up with pat answers and solutions. More often, they simply need us to listen and let them talk. That's the way God made them.

Spend as much time as you can with your mother. Weave her into the fabric of your life. Include her in your family activities whenever possible. I realize that your first priorities are your wife and children, but watching over your mother is not far behind.

Encourage her to have friends. Your mother needs to share her life with other people. She has much to offer and is a good companion and prayer partner. Encourage her to get out and do things, to meet new people, and to continue to develop and nurture her existing relationships. Make sure she isn't sitting home all the time, missing out on the full life she should be living.

Share your mother's interests. Don't expect her to share yours exclusively. Make sure she knows that the things that are important to her are also important to you.

Tell your mother *often* that you love her, and let her know your love is unconditional. Be sure that your children frequently tell their grandmother how much they love her, too. The words "I love you" are easy to say, but not said nearly enough. Never leave your mother or hang up from talking to her on the phone without saying those important words.

Encourage your mother and your children to spend time with each other. She can be a wonderful influence on them. The more time they spend together, the richer all of their lives will be.

Make sure your children always respect their grandmother. Brag about her often, lift her up in your children's esteem, and never say anything that might put her in a disparaging light in their eyes.

Maintain family traditions that are important to your mother. If these customs do not yet seem significant to you now, they may be one day. And even if some of them will never make it into your family's routine, show respect to your mother by honoring them anyway for her sake.

When God gave Moses the Ten Commandments, He divided them into two sections. The first four address our relationship to God. The last six focus on our relationships with one another. The first commandment of that second group tells us to honor our fathers and our mothers. This command is repeated in the New Testament. In Ephesians 6:1-3, God promises a long life to those who honor their parents. As eager as I am for you to join me, I would love to see you live a long, happy life on earth before you begin eternity here.

Your mother has always taken excellent care of you. Now is the time for role reversal. With me gone, it is your job to look out for her.

No one has ever done more for you than your mother. Now it is time for you to do your best for her. I know you won't let me down.

I love you, Son.

Dad

Chapter 5

What Would Dad Say About Family?

> Your wife and children will portray to others
> much the same image as you portray to them.

Dear Son,

You know how important our family was to me on earth. Well, now that I have a complete understanding of God's plan for mankind, my appreciation for the institution of family is even greater.

The Bible is filled with spiritual comparisons to the family. The first person of the Trinity is God the *Father.* The second is Jesus Christ, God's only begotten *Son.* When we accept Christ, we become adopted *children* of God, joint heirs with Christ. Together we are called the *family* of God, *brothers and sisters* with each other.

When God created the human race, He started with a family. He made Eve immediately after Adam and encouraged them to start having children right away.

The family is not only one of the first things God created, but also one of the most important. It is the entity that nurtures and protects people, gives them strength when they are weak, and encourages them through difficulties. It is also the venue God created to help people celebrate good times and to give them a framework from which to create the best aspects of life.

While most people would say they value their families, they often prove otherwise by their daily actions. In fact, they usually treat total strangers better than their wives or children. Many people put even themselves above their family. Unfortunately, they're missing out on one of the greatest blessings people on earth have available to them: the protection and unconditional acceptance of their loved ones.

Make time for your wife and children. No other ministry God could give you is more important than they are.

I mentioned to David the other day that I was going to talk to you about family, and he asked me to stress the importance of spending time with them. As you know, the Bible calls David "a man after God's own heart," and now that I've met him I can sure say *Amen* to that! This guy has more love for the Lord than just about anyone I've ever met, and that's saying a lot from up here.

But David got so wrapped up in serving God while he was living there on earth that he neglected his own family. He danced and sang praises to Jehovah, he spent lots of time in personal prayer and reflection, he led his people into battles to spread the Kingdom of God. He was the ultimate spiritual warrior and leader of his countrymen.

But his family took a backseat. To begin with, David had multiple wives. Although that was a commonly practiced custom at the time, this made it difficult for him to spend quality time with any one of them. When you try to divide your attention between multiple priorities, each one only gets a little bit of you, and everyone suffers.

David left the day-to-day raising of his children to his wives, their mothers. He was too busy expanding God's kingdom and praising the Lord for His bountiful mercies to be bothered with wiping noses, changing diapers, and bandaging scraped knees. He had kingly duties to attend to, worship services to organize, national disputes to settle. He attended military strategy meetings instead of his children's birthday celebrations. He made important political decisions rather than helping his wives decide how best to discipline the children when they misbehaved.

And David's children misbehaved *a lot*. So did most of his wives. For a true wakeup call, you can read all about it in the book of Second Samuel. It starts with David's coronation and his conquests. But chapters 12 through 20 show the devastating consequences of David's neglect of his family. His children rebelled against him and against God. The irony is, David's family conflicts resulted in disorder in the kingdom and revolt from the people David strived so hard to serve.

David realizes now that the sinful deeds of his wives and children were really cries for attention from a man too busy with good, wholesome, important activities to notice that his family was falling apart.

Some of David's wives and children are here with him in heaven. Others are not.

While there is no true sorrow here, David's heart still

grieves. Each of his family members made his or her own individual choice, but David realizes now that he could have influenced those choices to a much more powerful degree if only he'd spent more time with his family.

The most important thing you can do for your loved ones is to give them the spiritual foundation they will need to weather the storms of life. Spend time with each family member every day, praying, reading the Bible, and discussing God's Word. Go to church together every week. Read Christian books together. Invite Christian friends to your home often for fun and fellowship. Make your faith as vital a part of living as eating and breathing.

Plan holiday and birthday celebrations that everyone will enjoy. Maintain your own unique traditions. They will strengthen your family bonds and create strong, positive memories for years to come. Just be sure the traditions remain a tool to make your family stronger, not a burden that becomes a begrudged ritual.

Develop camaraderie among your family that is unbreakable by anyone or anything. Honor your wife and children and teach them how to honor one another.

Try to keep your family on the same timetable as much as possible. Eat in the same room (one without a television), go to bed at the same time, attend church as a family. Go out of your way to participate in activities together, rather than separately. You are not just a group of individuals who live under the same roof. You are a family.

Occasionally, people or circumstances will hurt the

members of your family. Comfort your wife and children when they are hurting. Be understanding. Be a good listener when they need one.

Make your home a safe haven from the outside world. Be sure your family members know you will not criticize, ridicule, or condemn them, and that you will not allow them to criticize, ridicule, or condemn one another. Accept them, and value each of them as an individual as well as a member of the family. Always remember, God is the one who joined you all together.

Some people think that if only they could change their family circumstances, their lives would be much better off. Children often want different parents. A wife may wish she had married someone else. A man might wonder what his life would be like if he had taken up with a different woman. This type of thinking is not only futile, but dangerous. These are the kind of musings that lead to adultery, divorce, runaways, and even suicide.

There may be certain extreme circumstances in which a person must separate himself and/or one of his family members from the others for the personal safety of all involved. But most of the time, we simply need to trust God to work through us within the circumstances in which we find ourselves.

Don't ever look at another family with envy, thinking their home life is "perfect." If there's one thing I've learned up here, it's that there's no such thing as a normal family. If you knew them as intimately as God does, you would realize that every single family on earth has quirks, black sheep, and secrets.

Strive to make your family the best it can be, but don't try to be perfect. Accept your family for what it is, warts and all.

Allow your family members to fail, and be forgiving when they do. Make sure everyone knows you are there to support them, and they are there to support each other. Remind them that failure does not change your family bond. You will also need to allow your wife and children to support you when you fail. That may be the most difficult task of all.

When things go awry, initiate a reconciliation as quickly as possible. Don't let the sun set on a broken family tie. Do whatever you can to make things right. If necessary, humble yourself and "take the fall." Your family is too important to spend even one moment out of unity.

Keep the lines of communication open at all times. Don't let any member of your family shut himself off from the others. Se sure everyone is able to safely say whatever is on their minds. Try to understand what they are attempting to communicate.

Don't be "thin skinned" when family members express themselves in a way that you perceive to be directed at you. Give them the benefit of the doubt.

And don't be afraid when family members express differing opinions. Diversity makes you stronger. Enjoy the differences; don't get angry over them.

Acts 12:12-17 tells the story of Peter going straight to the home of a woman named Mary after an angel miraculously delivered him out of prison.

I met Mary the other day. She was a widow when this event happened. Mary was wealthy, with a house large enough to accommodate the entire Jerusalem congregation. Life was difficult for Christ's followers at that time. Herod Agrippa had imprisoned Peter and killed James, John's brother. Yet this brave woman offered her house to the first group of Christians at Jerusalem as a place to worship God and pray.

As a result of her courageous example, her son, John Mark, became a missionary, church leader, and the author of the second gospel. Through this young man, countless people have been led to Christ and are now enjoying eternity here.

Your example to your family will have far-reaching effects, for good (like Mary) or for bad (like David). Probably a little of both, because no one is perfect, and because God can cause good to come even from evil, since He is more powerful than Satan. But choose each day the example you wish to set for your family. Your wife and children will portray to others much the same image as you portray to them.

Keep in touch with your extended family. Though you may not see them often, they are still family, and they're important. Whenever you have the opportunity, attend family reunions and visit your distant relatives.

When you join me here, you will realize that every person who has ever lived is "related" to every other person who ever lived, because we are all children of God and descendants of Adam and Eve, as well as descendants of Noah. So you are much more closely related to your second cousin once removed and your great-aunt by marriage than you may think!

Son, I love our family more now than I ever have. Please make sure it stays strong, not just for each other, but also for me, and for all the generations who have preceded you. My grandparents, and your mother's grandparents, going back countless centuries are all up here rooting for you. They worked hard to keep the family together, and their struggles were no less difficult than yours are today. Please don't let us down.

Mostly, remain strong for God. He loves our family even more than all of us put together.

I love you, Son.

Dad

Chapter 6

What Would Dad Say About Kids?

> I continue to beseech God--here in heaven--on my grandchildren's behalf.

Dear Son,

I loved my grandchildren very much on earth, but I love them even more here in heaven. Each one is very precious to me.

God has a plan for every living person. If we listen for God's leading, He joyfully reveals that plan to us, one step at a time. I believe that your children, my grandchildren, are willing to do that. I look forward to seeing what God has planned for them. I don't have a clue exactly what that will entail, but I know for a fact that their lives are important in the eternal scheme of things.

I know you worry that I am missing out on my grandchildren's lives. But nothing could be further from the truth. Even though I'm not there in person with them, you can be sure that I have a front-row seat as I watch my grandchildren live out their lives. And, man, am I proud!

Last Saturday, I watched your daughter's baseball game. And Moses sat right next to me. Can you believe it? Moses!

(Actually, he is quite the sports fan.) I was rooting like crazy, especially when my granddaughter slid on her rump to catch that fly ball in the sixth inning. Moses even gave me a big high-five!

I also saw her throw her bat into the dugout when she missed that fastball and struck out in the bottom of the ninth. I felt her disappointment, and yours, when her team lost the game.

You couldn't see it at the time, and still don't realize it, but there was a great lesson in that loss for both you and her. I know you like your children to win. Who doesn't? But many times, the best lessons are learned in the losses.

I know it grieves you that your children don't have my influence in their daily lives. I also know that you think you'll have a more difficult time raising them without my support. But the truth is, you have it! Even though I can't be there on earth to support you, I continue to beseech God--- here in heaven--on my grandchildren's behalf. Not a day goes by that I don't approach God, directly and personally, to ask Him for protection and blessings for you and my grandchildren.

When I was on earth, I tried my best to be a good father to you. I know I wasn't perfect, but I hope I was an example that you can, at least partially, emulate with your children.

I tried to be supportive, but I never felt comfortable giving you parenting advice. I thought I should mind my own business and not meddle in yours. But, with my new perspective, there are some things that I'd like to share with you about your children. You might not have been completely open to my advice while I was on earth, but I suspect you'd like to hear what I have to say now!

First, you *must* make time for your children. There are no excuses for not spending time with your kids. They are your first priority, your most important ministry. Nothing in your life, besides your own relationship with God, is more important. And maintaining your relationship with your children is part of maintaining your relationship with God. He will never ask you to sacrifice them for any other ministry, occupation, or priority.

I've met several Bible heroes and other great men of faith up here who regret not having a better relationship with their children when they lived on earth. Some of them made great names for themselves, but lost their children for all eternity. They forgot their first ministry: their kids. And they regret it now.

I know you're busy, Son, but make sure you're never too busy to spend large quantities of time with your children. Play with them. Laugh with them. Hug them. Indulge them. Do with them all the things I can't, until they join me here.

Please give my grandchildren unconditional love. There will be times when they will disappoint you or embarrass you. Make sure they know they have your love, no matter what they do. Tell them, repeatedly, how much you love them, and that you will never stop loving them.

And tell them Granddad loves them, too!

Accept your children for who they are, as God designed them. Pick your fights carefully. As long as your children's clothing is modest, don't argue over style. Whether you want to believe it or not, their opinions and preferences are just as important as yours! Make sure they know that.

Encourage them to find God's plan for their life, not your plan for them. Believe me, Son, no matter how noble your intentions are, God's plan for them is better. And He will only reveal it to them, not to you.

As the head of the household, you must establish family limits. Boundaries are very important for kids. Make sure yours know that the rules you set are to protect them, not confine them. Although most kids would never admit it, they really do prefer reasonable rules. It provides them the freedom to act within the boundaries, and feel safe within them.

Always base your rules on sound principles you can describe and defend. Arbitrary regulations only lead to bitterness and rebellion.

Make sure your children know that their importance is not based on conformity to rules, but on their worth as God's creations. While you may disagree with their opinions or actions, your love for them must be unconditional.

Remember, rules that are good for some of the family are good for all of the family. If your children see you cheating on your taxes, how can you tell them not to cheat on their tests? If you bring home paperclips from the office, you diminish your authority to tell them not to steal things from a store. On the other hand, if they see you consistently following Christ, they will quite naturally follow Him in their own lives.

Be your children's best friend. Foster a good relationship with each one of them. Without that, the rules and guidelines you lay out for them will mean absolutely nothing.

Don't exercise unnecessary control over your children. Give them autonomy as it is appropriate. Let each of them be his or her own person. Give them the tools to discern right from wrong, and then give them the opportunity to control themselves.

They won't handle this responsibility perfectly every time. I can guarantee you, they will fail once in a while. We all do. But they will never learn how to succeed if they are never given a chance to fail.

There will come a time when they will need their freedom. It will be hard for you to back off. I went through that with you. Don't take it personally when they pull away. It's a normal part of growing up.

Make sure the lines of communication stay open. Be a good listener, and try to understand what your children are saying. Don't feel like you have to be talking all the time.

When you do talk, choose your words carefully. Never make idle threats. Think before you speak, and be prepared to follow through on any promises, or consequences, you present to them.

Make sure your kids understand the importance of honesty. Never punish them if they have tried to be honest with you. This just encourages them to lie the next time a similar situation comes up. The best way to teach your children honesty is to be a man of your word to them. Make sure they know that if you tell them something, they can count on it!

Provide your children with goals that are high, but not beyond their ability to reach. Keep the kids busy in constructive activities, and give them objectives within those activities that are just within their grasp. When they reach those goals, praise them unabashedly.

For every one thing your children need correction for, there are probably twenty-five things they should be praised for. Positive reinforcement is a powerful tool. Praise your children a lot more than you criticize them. Catch them doing things right, and let them know you appreciate what they have done.

Finally, the most important thing you can give your children is a strong spiritual base. It is imperative that they learn about God, and it is your responsibility, and privilege, to teach them.

Some parents think their kids should choose for themselves whether they want to learn about God and follow Him. That's crazy! You don't let your children choose for themselves in other areas of life, do you?

Remember when your teenager wanted to stay up until midnight on a school night? Or that Fourth of July when your two year old pouted and cried because you wouldn't let him shoot off fireworks? How many times did the kids try to get out of school by pretending to be sick, when you knew the real reason was that they hadn't finished their homework or studied for an important test? How about the time that feisty little granddaughter of mine wanted a fourth helping of chocolate cake, when you could tell the first three were probably going to make her sick?

In any of those instances, did you simply say, "Do whatever you want to, Honey. Whatever you choose to do is fine with me." Of course not! You understood that they need guidance in these areas.

Guidance is even more important when it comes to the spiritual aspect of their lives. In fact, this is the most important thing you can do for your children.

The psychologists up here generally agree that the ages between sixteen and twenty-two are the most important years of a child's life. During that time, they make many key decisions that will affect them, either positively or negatively, for the rest of their lives. They will either reap the rewards or pay the price for those decisions *forever.* Of course, you should help your children make good decisions throughout their lives. But be especially supportive during these years when they come.

Son, I know you love your kids and want the best for them. I do, too. But always remember that God's love for your children surpasses yours and mine put together, if you can imagine that!

I love you, Son.

Dad

Chapter 7

What Would Dad Say About People?

You can tell very little about a person's
heart by his or her outward appearance.

Dear Son,

People matter a great deal to God. They should also matter to you. Every person, regardless of his or her background, is important because God made them all.

People are different, but that doesn't mean some are right and others are wrong. Don't think less of someone because he is different from you in any way. Value the differences and learn from them.

One way in which people are different is their culture. Don't stand in judgment of other races, methods of governing, or economic systems. Try to understand the background and histories of countries unlike your own without characterizing or stereotyping them. Respect others and deal with them as individuals.

I was sitting at the banquet table the other day (I couldn't really tell you which day it was--time doesn't mean much up here), enjoying a truly heavenly meal with the Lord. (The food was so delicious I couldn't possibly describe it in earthly words, so I won't even try!) Anyway, I met this great guy named Wally. He and I became friends quickly. (Then again, that happens to everyone here since we now see each other as Christ sees us.) Wally told me he spent most of his life on earth being judgmental and critical of other people. Now he looks back and wonders why in the world he wasted his energy like that!

"I could have done so many positive things with my life," Wally told me, shaking his head. "But for some reason, I chose to tear people down instead of building them up."

The earth is full of poverty and heartache. People everywhere continue to pay the price for original sin every day. (By the way, I asked Adam and Eve what they were thinking when they ate that fruit. I'll let them tell you themselves when you get here.)

As an ambassador for Christ, help people with their physical and emotional needs. Show them the light that shines from within you.

Be thankful that you are one of the lucky few who live a comfortable life. But always remember that most of the world does not live like you do. Even those in America who are considered poor are living in luxury compared to folks in many foreign countries. You had no control over the fact that you were born into a Christian family in America. Don't hold anything against anyone who isn't so fortunate.

Show compassion and empathy toward others. Take time to visualize how you would feel, and would want to be treated, if you were one of the unfortunate ones. Imagine living in a cardboard box and not knowing where your next meal is coming from. Try to put yourself in their place. It will make you a much better person.

People who seem cold or cruel have their own problems. Many times, they are acting out how they have been treated during a previous time in their life. Try to be cheerful and gracious toward everyone, even those who are not kind to you.

Another new friend of mine here is Sally. She had an incredibly difficult life on earth. She suffered abuse as a child, then lost her husband in the military when she was just twenty-three. She had no other family and no friends to speak of. She became bitter about her experiences and spent the next four decades wallowing in unhappiness.

Do you know why Sally looked me up when she got here? Because your mother met her at a doctor's office one day and befriended her. Mom was the first person in years who'd spoken kind words of unconditional concern for her. While most of the world considered Sally just a bitter, miserable old lady, one person was able to change her life around by showing her a few moments of kind attention. Little things matter when you are dealing with people.

If you find yourself in a position to show mercy to someone, do it. Remember, Jesus said, "Blessed are the merciful."

Don't judge or condemn others. The people who are the most judgmental often have the least right to be. Judgmental people are usually the most miserable.

For true happiness and self-improvement, focus on what you can control (yourself) instead of what you can't (others).

When you focus on yourself, your area of influence actually increases.

Don't let other people control you, either. What others say shouldn't impact you. It's pointless to let someone's words or actions make you unhappy. Don't get worked up by the foolish dealings of others. Remember, what you see and feel and experience are just temporary circumstances of life. Take your eyes off those circumstances and place them on things above, on the eternal things that will never pass away.

Don't let yourself be eaten up by grudges. Enmity toward others will affect you in many ways. Turn the other cheek. Life is too short to worry about actions others take, no matter how egregious they may appear to you.

Jesus said, "Blessed are the peacemakers." Avoid conflict and promote peace whenever you can. Others will have different perspectives from yours. Instead of engaging in arguments, try to appreciate the other viewpoint.

Remember, it is the inside that matters. You can tell very little about a person's heart by his or her outward appearance.

This principle works both ways. One man may talk about all the wonderful things he does, but be exceedingly wicked inside. Another may have a heart that longs for God, but also have facets of his appearance you find objectionable. Only God knows the heart, so don't waste even one moment of your time trying to figure it out. You will either be very wrong or very tired!

Dealing with others can be complex and difficult, but God

has given you the keys to living the abundant life. Jesus made His desire clear in His command for us to love one another. The golden rule, which originated from Jesus Himself, tells us to treat others as we would want to be treated.

Remember the other day when that lady ahead of you in line at the cash register offered to let you go ahead of her? You were running late for an appointment, and thanks to her, you made it on time. (You didn't know I saw that, did you?) Doesn't it feel wonderful when someone does something kind? Well, every day, you have countless opportunities to make others feel the same way. It's not difficult to extend a helping hand, a loving action, or a kind word.

Strive to make sure that every person you come in contact with is more lifted up, more encouraged, and less burdened than before your meeting. People remember those who, by virtue of their presence and conversation, brought them to a higher plane in life.

And when you get up here, Jesus Himself will commend you for every moment you spent making someone else's day a little brighter. I'm looking forward to sitting in the audience watching that, bragging to everyone within earshot, "That's my boy!" On that day, as you look back on those tiny, seemingly insignificant moments, you will realize that there was nothing more important you could have spent that time doing.

I love you, Son.

Dad

Chapter 8

What Would Dad Say About Fear?

> There is only one thing people truly should fear,
> and that is spending eternity without God.

Dear Son,

You may find this hard to believe, but did you know fear is actually a gift from God? It's true! In its original intended form, fear is a protective emotion that our loving heavenly Father created to help people deal with times of real trouble. It's good to have a "healthy fear" of things like hot stoves and poisonous snakes and falling off a cliff.

Trouble is, some folks seem to live in a constant state of fear or nervousness about *something*. And most people fear all the wrong things. For example:

- People fear other people. Some folks think of themselves as inferior to, or less valuable than, those around them. They're afraid others might know things they don't, things that could hurt them. On the other hand, some folks seem to think they're a great deal better than others, and they worry that association with people who are less important than they are might somehow diminish their chances for success.

The fact is, people are all basically the same. Each of us is made in the image of God. No matter what our position in life, we all have similar wants, needs, and insecurities. Heaven is filled with people, and lots more come in every single day. But I have yet to see one person who is any better or worse than anyone else. We're all just a bunch of saved sinners up here.

So don't fear people. Love and support them the best you can. Otherwise, you'll miss out on myriad relationships that can enrich your time on earth in countless ways.

- People fear the loss of material possessions. Or worse, poverty itself. A lot of folks depend on their possessions to give them a sense of personal identity. They believe the loss of their worldly goods will reduce their self- worth. In reality, their value as a person has nothing to do with how much they own.

Very little of what you possess today will still be yours twenty years from now, much less a hundred years. So don't place value on things that are temporary. I guarantee you, within seconds of arriving here in heaven, you will realize how silly it was to be consumed with obtaining and protecting your earthly belongings.

- People fear speaking up. It's normal to feel nervous about sharing your faith with others who may disagree with what you believe. But don't give into that fear, or you will lose many opportunities to bring others closer to Christ. Speak up for what you believe, even when doing so is uncomfortable.

Many years before my transition from earth to heaven, I met a man named Joe who was truly hostile about the things of the Lord. His mother was a member of our congregation, and one day she asked if I would pay Joe a visit to speak to him about the Lord. I agreed, although somewhat reluctantly. To be quite honest, I was afraid of what that man's reaction would be.

As I approached Joe's house I felt my knees literally shaking with fear. When he opened the door, I expected him to slam it right in my face. To my surprise, he cordially invited me in. When I started speaking to him about his relationship with God, he actually listened. Imagine my astonishment when, moments later, Joe told me he was ready to invite Christ to be Lord of his life!

On the way home I thought to myself, "This must be a dream ... or maybe Joe had too much to drink and didn't know what he was doing!" But the next Sunday, there he was--in church--with his family and his God-fearing mother.

I lost track of Joe a few years later, but I've been watching his life from up here, and do you know, he hasn't missed church a single Sunday since that day. In fact, he stopped drinking, stepped down from his family-owned business, enrolled in Bible college, and today is an ordained minister of the gospel. Talk about a radical change! And to think that fear almost prevented me from having that talk with him.

Never allow fear to keep you from doing what you know you should. God will be there, right alongside you, even inside you, speaking through you the words He knows others need to hear.

- People fear embarrassment. A lot of folks here, when they look back on their lives on earth, realize that they missed out on many opportunities to accomplish great things, simply because they were afraid of being embarrassed.

What if Noah had been too embarrassed to build the ark? The entire human race would have been wiped out in the flood. What if Joshua had been too embarrassed to walk around those walls? Or David too embarrassed to stand up to Goliath? I could go on forever (literally!) with examples of great things that were accomplished because people were not afraid of being embarrassed. Don't let this fear keep you from doing something big with your life.

- People fear the unknown. Son, when you were born, *everything* was unknown to you. As you grew older, you experienced many "firsts." Once you became acquainted with and accustomed to these new activities, you . learned what to expect. They were no longer unknown, so they ceased to cause you any fear.

You still haven't experienced everything. There will always be some "unknowns." What will life be like when your kids are teenagers, or when they move out of the house and have families of their own? How will it feel to grow old? To retire? To be a granddad? I could tell you what these things were like for me, but God alone knows how your life will turn out.

But that's the good news! The future is unknown to you, yet nothing ever surprises God. He knows everything. You can trust Him and not be afraid.

- People fear change. As a matter of fact, most folks are terrified of it! But in the vast majority of instances, change is a wonderful thing. You learn a lot more from change that you do from living in a rut.

So embrace change. See it as an opportunity for growth.

For several years I kept my eyes peeled for the right girl to be my bride. She had to be a perfect 10, inside and out! Over the years I did more than my share of dating, but couldn't seem to find Miss Right. It seemed that each girl I dated was lacking something.

Then one day someone suggested I stop looking at the girls' faults and begin focusing on my own. This friend suggested, "Maybe the reason you're not married yet is that you're not ready to be the kind of husband God desires for your mate." That thought blew me away! Talk about a change in perspective! My friend even suggested I put a hold on dating for a while and do some serious praying! What a radical concept! For some reason, it had never occurred to me to make my marriage a matter of serious prayer. So, instead of trying to take charge of my future, I threw everything I knew about dating out the window and took the matter to God. For weeks I spent my evening meal times in prayer rather than eating (one of my favorite pastimes). I found a lonely park in Pomona, California, and each night I just walked and prayed.

My prayer went something like this: "Lord, please make me a good partner for the girl you have picked out to be my wife. I'm kind of in a hurry, but I'm willing to wait until you say the time is right. Please work on me, and when I'm ready, just point me in the right direction and I'll take it from there."

Would you believe less than four months later I was married to the girl of my dreams! The twist of irony is that, years earlier, I had fired this girl from a ministry position. In fact, she's the only person I've ever fired! When the Lord told me she was the one, I thought, "Are you sure?" But the Lord was certain. He doesn't make mistakes.

I thank God for changing my perspective on marriage. That incident helped me embrace change, seeing it as a tool God often uses to mold us into the people He wants us to be!

- People fear failure. No one sets out to intentionally fail. Everyone wants to succeed. But the truth is, we learn more from our failures than we do from our successes. When things go the way we hoped and planned, we tend to pat ourselves on the back, become overconfident, and feel pretty self-sufficient. But when we are discouraged because the things we attempted did not work out the way we anticipated, we turn to God. Humbled, we realize that we can accomplish nothing that is truly important without His help.

When we acknowledge our dependence on Him, He does not respond by chastising us for our failures, or even encouraging us to try harder next time so we can have more successes and fewer failures. No, He reminds us of Philippians 4:13, "I can do all things through Christ who strengthens me." He can use even your failures for His glory!

- People fear death. This is a major concern for most folks. Some are absolutely consumed with the thought of it. But death is simply a transition from a mortal, earthly existence to the immortal life of eternity.

   It is said that the only certainties in life are death and taxes. Well, Son, a few people may get away with cheating on their taxes, but no one can cheat death. So why spend your life being afraid of something everyone experiences, sooner or later.

There is only one thing people truly should fear, and that is spending eternity without God. Son, hell is real, and it is more frightening than you can possibly imagine! If people on earth had even a tiny glimpse of this gruesome reality, they would run straight into the arms of their loving heavenly Father and beg Him to save them from it, no matter what the cost.

But thanks be to God, He has already paid the cost for our salvation from an eternity in hell. For those who have accepted Christ's substitutionary death on the cross, the future holds absolutely nothing to fear.

Think back over your life. Remember the things you worried about five, ten, fifteen years ago? In retrospect, do you realize that you never really needed to be afraid? How many of the things you feared actually came to pass? Of those that did, how many resulted in dire consequences of the magnitude you imagined?

Now, apply this principle to your life today. In five or ten years, don't you think you'll look back on the things you fear today and realize that your worry was completely unfounded? If so, discard your fears and be liberated. I'm sure you can find more important things to spend your time doing!

With the benefit of hindsight, I realize now that all of my fears on earth were unnecessary. God did not allow anything to come to pass in my life that He did not approve ahead of time. And not one single moment of fear, nervousness, or worry on my part changed a thing!

Someday, you will be here with me, and you will see how silly it was to fear things on earth. Instead of waiting until that day, I hope you'll use this knowledge to make your life better now. Just keep· in mind what the angels always said whenever they appeared to someone on earth.

"Fear not!"

I love you, Son.

Dad

Chapter 9

What Would Dad Say About Grace?

> As He has shown you grace, be sure to
> show grace to those around you.

Dear Son,

Grace ... how I love the sound of that word!

Grace means "undeserved favor." It signifies gifts of love poured out upon others, gifts that are entirely undeserved. Like that baseball mitt your mother and I gave you for your tenth birthday, even though you were grounded at the time.

Since I arrived in heaven, I've come to understand that God is even more rich in grace and mercy than I ever imagined. You wouldn't believe how much this place is filled with the aroma and evidence of it!

I also understand that mercy and grace are not the same thing. Mercy involves *not* receiving something *bad* that you deserve. Grace is a matter of receiving something *good* that you do *not* deserve. Fortunately for us, our Father God is rich in both.

I know you always thought I was a pretty good guy, and I did try to do my best at all times, especially for my family.

I made every attempt to live an honorable life, and to be a devoted husband and faithful father. But now that I'm here, I realize how puny even my greatest, most valiant human efforts were. I could never be "good enough" to deserve to be allowed entrance here.

When I approached the Eastern gate, not one single soul asked me for a list of my accomplishments or good deeds. I was asked just one question, and I answered by giving my name. When it was found in the Lamb's Book of Life, I was instantly ushered through the gate. It really was that simple!

When I lived on earth, I could recite every single Bible verse about salvation being by grace, not by works. And I believed every word. But back there, works were easier to see. Grace was a far more intangible concept.

It's the exact opposite here. No one sees anyone else's works. But grace is evident everywhere you look!

The only reason I'm in heaven right now is because of His grace. You know, God would have been justified in placing me for eternity into a steaming hot jungle or an ice-covered deep freeze. Instead, He made me the crown jewel of His creation and placed me right smack dab in the middle of heaven!

And this city is absolutely breathtaking. Sometimes, I pinch myself to make sure I'm not dreaming. I often think to myself, "I don't deserve to live in a place like this." But that's the whole point! I'm not here because I earned the right to be. I'm here only because of His grace. You see, heaven--and life itself, for that matter--is all about grace.

Did you know, by God's grace, I'm actually part owner of this fabulous place! Do you remember Saint Paul

writing, "We are heirs and co-heirs with Christ"? It's true! As a child of God, heaven is not just where I live, it's what I own. Now, that's grace!
John the disciple wrote that God made us to be kings and that we will reign forever. Well, guess what? Your old dad is now a reigning king. How about that? As a child of God, I am one of many who rule and reign over God's universe!

Not bad for a guy who started out climbing telephone poles for AT&T, huh? If anyone ever started at the "bottom of the ladder," it was me. (Remember that time I was chased up a telephone pole by wild boars, or when I had to avoid stepping on rattlesnakes while repairing downed wires?)

If you had told me back then that I would one day rule and reign over all creation alongside the Almighty Himself, I would have said you were crazy! Yet here I am. How do I explain it? It's all grace.

Remember when we used to sing, "Amazing Grace"? I always loved that hymn. But I really didn't have a clue what I was singing, or just how amazing God's grace really is. Now I understand.

The first person I met when I arrived here was, of course, the Lord Jesus Himself. We talked for ... well, I don't really know how long, because time is irrelevant here. But as we looked back over my life, I was astonished to discover that the incidents that seemed to matter most to Him were times I barely even noticed or remembered.

Jesus reminded me, for example, of that single gal in our church who was having a tough time a few years ago. Her husband had deserted her, leaving her to raise two children alone. The poor thing had it rough and your mother and I felt sorry for her. We loved sharing what we had with her.

I remember thinking, "If something happened to me, and my wife was left alone, I'd want someone to take notice and be there to help her."

Now, I didn't do all that much for this little lady. If she needed a screen replaced or a section of her roof repaired, I'd take care of it for her. If we saw her kids needed some clothes or school supplies, we'd try to help. Since she had no car and we had two, we sometimes loaned her our second car so she could get around. Of course, we always filled the gas tank for her.

Would you believe those small acts of grace really touched Jesus' heart? He told me, "In caring for her, you cared for Me. In giving to her, you gave to Me." I'm not certain, but I think I saw a tear in His eye as he told me how much it meant to Him that we took pity on some fatherless children.

Now, there's a lesson here for you. As a child of the King, the all-gracious One, you should also be known for your gracious spirit toward others. As He has shown you grace, be sure to show grace to those around you.

Be kind to everyone. Life is, at best, difficult--at worst, brutal. People all around you are hurting and struggling. Look at them through the eyes of your Savior. Care for them, be kind to them, and show them grace.

Don't fight over the best parking spot at the mall. Let the other driver have it. Park out where no one else is parked. You'll get fewer dings in your car, the walk will be good for your heart, and you will brighten someone's day. You will be, in effect, walking in the grace of God.

If you want to put a smile on Jesus' face, be kind to

everyone. Don't get angry and don't get even. Instead, offer grace. Don't step on others to get ahead. Step up to them and give them grace. Don't do unto others before they can do unto you. Extend grace. Don't say, "I'll forgive you, but I'll never forget what you did." With grace, cover what they did and let it go.

Grace always attempts to reconcile broken relationships. Life is too short to hold onto grudges. Forgive just as God has forgiven you. And before you reply, "But Dad, they don't deserve it," remember ... neither do you! Yet God forgave you anyway. That's grace. So be like Christ and do the same.

Grace always gives others the benefit of the doubt. It never stands in harsh judgment. Grace never takes; it always gives, and always much more than is merited.

Let your children see grace in the way you deal with their mother and in the way you respond to them. Let them see grace in all you do. Don't just be gracious to them; teach them to be gracious to others.

The best example of grace I can offer you is that of Jesus Himself. Even before He was nailed to a cross, people spit on Him. They slapped Him around. They pulled His beard. They blindfolded Him and struck Him. They pressed a crown of thorns deep into His brow. They scourged Him with a whip.

After the scourging, Jesus was forced to carry His own cross to Mount Calvary. Once there, He was stripped naked and nailed to a tree. He hung in agony for six hours. He endured thirst and heat while the crowd laughed and jeered at Him. He was called a liar and an impostor. (Can you imagine? Jesus Christ was accused of blasphemy!) He struggled for every breath. He was forced to look down into the tear-stained face of His precious mother, who died a thousand deaths as she watched Him hang on that cross.

The sins of all time were laid upon Him and, as a result, for the first and only time in all history, the Son of God was separated from the Father He loved and who loved Him.

Yet, having endured all this, He looked into the faces of the angry mob and said, "Father, forgive them, for they know not what they do."

Now, that's grace.

If I had my earthly life to live over again, I believe the one area in which I would concentrate more would be in living a life of grace. I hope you'll meditate upon God's unlimited grace and attempt to live your life with His grace always uppermost in your mind.

I love you, Son.

Dad

Chapter 10

What Would Dad Say About Choices?

> Circumstances are often the direct
> consequences of our choices.

Dear Son,

Many people go through life wondering why good things never happen to them, why they can't ever seem to "catch a break." Those people are missing one of life's greatest principles: Circumstances are often the direct consequences of our choices.

A person's life situation is usually the result of two things:

1. all the decisions they have made up to that point, and
2. all the actions they have taken related to those decisions.

While you have the freedom to choose your behavior, you have no control over the consequences of the behavior you have chosen. This dates back to Adam and Eve. No one is exempt from it, and you cannot change it. The best thing to do is acknowledge this principal and respect it.

Unfortunately, most people never make the connection between their past actions and their current state of affairs.

Since they are unable to see that connection, they don't realize that their future will be a direct result of their actions today. They think "fate," or some other factor outside their control, determines what will happen to them. When their life flies out of control, they truly do not understand why.

The good news is that this principal works just as potently concerning good decisions as it does for bad ones. If you make right choices, you will reap the benefits for years to come.

Remember how hard you worked in college--especially with all those math classes? Many times, you turned down fun social activities to spend time studying for exams. Today you're reaping the benefits of getting a good education. You need to continue improving yourself daily. This will ensure that you have the skills necessary to deal with whatever issues develop later on.

Please make sure my grandchildren understand this concept. It is one of the most important principles you can teach them. If they grasp the connection between their behavior and its consequences, they will be more likely to make choices that will have a positive impact on their lives.

Your decisions also affect the people who are close to you. You may think you are the only one who will suffer if you make a bad decision. But I guarantee you, it will also impact your family and friends. When you're considering an important decision, think about those who are closest to you and how the consequences of your decision will affect their lives.

Let me point out some specific areas in which you can apply this principle to your life today.

- Your wife. Your first priority is to the mate God has given you. Choose to spend time every day improving your relationship with her. When everyone else disappoints you, you'll want your relationship with her to be strong. She is the mother of your children, and the one who will grow old with you, so don't invest in other relationships at her expense. Most of the success or failure people experience in their lives is a direct result of happiness or sadness in their marital relationships. Make your future happier by investing in your wife. Start today!
- Your children. My grandchildren's futures depend on how much you invest in them today. Don't let distractions prevent you from spending time with them. Believe me, the years go by quickly. Soon, your children will have their own lives and you will long for more time with them. Ensure a happier future for your children--and yourself--by investing liberally in their lives today.
- Your friends. Good friends are hard to find. Continue to nurture your current friendships and be on the lookout for new relationships that can be a source of support for you and your family. Remember David and Jonathan from the Old Testament? They are as inseparable now as they were back in Saul's day! Not even death could separate those two.
- Other people. When you have the resources and ability to do so, help others generously. Don't be afraid that someone might take advantage of you.

Take the risk, and trust God for the results. I ran into the innkeeper who offered Mary and Joseph the use of his stable for Jesus' birth. You wouldn't believe how dramatically that man's life changed from the moment he chose to perform that one simple act of kindness.

- Yourself. Choose to spend time every day in focused prayer, studying your Bible, reading other good books, and taking additional steps to improve yourself. Never stop learning about the things that are important.

I know you've made some bad decisions in the past---everyone has. And chances are, you will again. But don't get discouraged. Just do whatever you can to get yourself back on the right path. Ask forgiveness of God and the people whose lives have been affected by your wrong choices. Analyze the circumstances that led up to the moment where you veered off course, but only long enough to determine how you can avoid making the same mistake again. Then move on, confident that God will help you make the right decisions if you diligently seek His guidance.

You cannot change the past, but you can affect the future. Take the right steps today to ensure that you will reap the rewards in years to come.

You've already made the best decision any person can make: You've accepted Jesus Christ as your personal Savior. Believe me, the rewards that await you here are beyond description!

I love you, Son.

Dad

Chapter 11

What Would Dad Say About Right and Wrong?

> One of the devil's favorite tricks is
> convincing us to question whether God's
> Word really means what it seems to.

Dear Son,

Upon arriving here in heaven, one of the first things that impressed me about our Creator was His perfection. He is perfectly pure, just, holy, and righteous. He has no dark side. He is above reproach in every way. His integrity is impeccable. He's completely honest. There is absolutely no deceit in Him.

You have heard it's impossible for God to lie. Well, that's no lie! He is incapable of deception. When He referred to Himself as "the Truth," He was telling the truth. He always does right, and He never does wrong.

People, on the other hand, often struggle in this area of right and wrong. I did, and I know you do too.

Some people believe everyone should make their own rules as they go along, that individuals have the authority to determine what is right and wrong for them. They may not realize it, but in doing so, they actually deify themselves--

they become their own gods. When you get here, you will realize how silly that is!

So how does a person determine whether something is right or wrong? What basis or standard can be used to guide us to the right path?

The only inerrant authority is the Holy Bible. You will never go wrong by following and obeying its precepts.

The guidelines set forth in the Bible are not there to constrain you. On the contrary, they will protect you and give you freedom. Even when you do not understand the reasons for God's rules, trust Him and follow them.

Many believers become confused because they read the Bible with preconceived notions. Christians are notorious for twisting the Scripture to say whatever they want it to say.

Remember how sin started, in the Garden? Satan whispered in Eve's ear, "Has God indeed said, 'You shall not eat of every tree of the garden'?"

She knew what God had told them. There was no question about it. "You shall not eat it, nor shall you touch it, lest you die."

But when Satan told her, "You will not surely die," she took the fruit and ate it. Satan deceived her into questioning the obvious direction God had given.

From that day to this, one of the devil's favorite tricks is convincing us to question whether God's Word really means what it seems to. Trust me, Son--it does!

Rather than allowing your preferences, convictions, traditional beliefs, and personal desires shape your understanding of the Scriptures, let God's Word impact and influence you.

I will never forget the wonderful night when your mother led me to Christ. It happened many years ago, before you were born. A friend of your mom's had spent time with her that day, sharing with her how she could have her sins forgiven. Your mother accepted Christ as her Savior right then and there.

Later that evening, your mother was so excited. She could hardly wait to tell me what had happened to her. She opened her Bible and shared the same Scriptures with me that her friend had shared with her. Before the night was over, she had pointed me to Christ too.

From the moment I accepted Christ as my Lord, there was an immediate change in my life. When I took Christ as my Savior, I made up my mind to please Him and obey His Word. The way I saw it, if He could die for me, I could live for Him. I decided to accept the Bible at face value and just do what it said to do. Son, I want you to do the same. Obey the Book!

You will sometimes be faced with situations the Bible does not specifically address. When that happens, just ask yourself what Jesus would do in the same circumstances. If you spend time getting to know Him and His character well, you will be able to anticipate how He would respond, and then do the same yourself.

You can also ask yourself, "Of all the options I have before me, which will bring the most honor to God?" Chances are, the answer to that question will provide you with the information you need to make the right decision.

If you're not certain what Jesus would do, or which move would most honor God, take some time to pray about the matter. Ask the Holy Spirit to lead you, to direct you to God's will.

God never tries to hide or disguise His will. He will not play cosmic hide-and-seek with you. He wants you to know and do His will, even more than you want to know and do it. If you sincerely seek Him, He will make His will clear to you. So pray with a pure heart, motivated only by a desire to please Him. If you do, He will be quick to respond.

So, what do you do when you've done wrong? Here's the really good news. Your heavenly Father loves you so much that if you run to Him, like the prodigal son, He will forgive you immediately and completely. Where sin abounds, His grace abounds even more. If you have an ounce of sin, He has a pound of grace. If you have a pound of sin, He has a ton of grace. If you have a ton of sin, He has truckloads of grace. Sin is finite; His grace is infinite.

And when God forgives, He also forgets. Completely. He separates our sin from His memory as far as the east is from the west. He cleanses us, literally washing our guilt away.

Son, can you ever remember a time when you asked for my forgiveness and I was not willing to grant it? Of course not. You never had to ask a second time. Well, you have a heavenly Father who loves you even more than I could ever begin to.

But how much better it is to choose the right path in the first place than to do wrong and have to ask forgiveness! Even though God forgives, freely and completely, sin still has its consequences, and sometimes they can be truly horrendous. Every person I run into up here (except Jesus, of course) can attest to that fact.

Keep your eyes on Jesus, and you'll always do right.

Follow the Bible's guidelines, and you'll never go wrong.
    I love you, Son.

                                      Dad

Chapter 12

What Would Dad Say About Foundations?

Whatever Jesus asks of you, make sure your answer is a resounding "Yes, Lord!"

Dear Son,

In His famous Sermon on the Mount, Jesus spoke about the importance of building your life upon a solid foundation. He told the story of a foolish man who built his house on the sand. When the storms came, the foolish man's house fell. The wise man, on the other hand, built his house on a rock. When the storms blew against it, his house stood firm. One of the primary reasons so many families are collapsing today is that they are built on the sinking sand of human effort. If you want stability in your life, your marriage, and your home, it is imperative that you build upon the proper foundations.

The first foundation is *God's Word.*

Most people today pay little attention to what the Bible has to say. Never forget--what you do with the Bible determines what God does with you.

The old adage is true, "The Bible will keep you from sin, or sin will keep you from the Bible." Let the Scriptures become a light to your feet and a lamp to your path. Hide God's words in your heart, and your family will be the better for it.

It is not enough to believe God's Word or even to read and study it. You must also obey it, following its instruction completely.

As I look back over my life, I can honestly say the Bible never led me wrong. Not once. I can think of many occasions where I did not follow the Scriptures, and regretted it. But I never regretted obeying them.

The second foundation to build your life upon is *love.*

The Lord gave Moses ten commandments, but Jesus gave His disciples an eleventh one, that they love one another. He told them the greatest of all the commandments was to love God, and second on the list was to love other people. If you obey these two commands, there's no need for any others.

If you love your wife, you'll take care of her, protect her, and treat her with honor and respect. If you love your children, you will be fair with them, kind to them, and always encourage them to do what's right. If you love your fellow man, you will never even contemplate taking advantage of, cheating, stealing from, or hurting him in any way. Those you come into contact with should be overwhelmed by the loving and gracious manner in which you treat them.

Fall in love with the Lord every day. Allow His love to flow through you to all those who know you. See to it that your home is, above all else, a place of unconditional and lasting love. Your children should never doubt your love for them. Your wife should be secure in your love for her.

Make your home a place where Jesus would feel comfortable. Establish every room with Him in mind. Ask yourself, "Is there anything that is seen, heard, or done in this room that does not please and honor Him?" If so, do some house cleaning. May your home be so dedicated to Him that, each time a guest enters your front door, he is immediately struck by the difference in your home.

Do you know why you and I had such a close relationship while I was on earth? It was not just because I was your dad. Many fathers and sons are not close. It was because we loved each other deeply. I loved you, and you loved me, and we both knew it.

Remember that time I drove halfway across the country to help you move out of your apartment following your college graduation? I had just had my second open- heart surgery and was in no condition to be going anywhere except to bed. Yet I changed a flat tire on 1-65, trying not to pull the stitches out of my chest, just so I could see the surprise in your eyes when I showed up on moving day. You couldn't believe I'd drive hundreds of miles to help you move your furniture. But the thought of staying put while my son needed help never occurred to me. I wanted to be there for you because I loved you. If ever a dad loved his son, I loved mine! And I wanted you to know it.

My entire life was devoted to our family. I hope you, too, will build your home on the foundation of love. If you do, it will become a little bit of heaven on earth, for more than anything else, heaven is a place of love.

The final foundation is *Jesus Christ Himself.*

Jesus is the Rock of ages and the Rock of your salvation. He is the Stone the builders rejected and the chief Cornerstone of the Church. In Him, there is security. He is strong. He never wavers. He never changes. What He was, He still is, and He always will be.

Everything you have ever heard about Jesus is an understatement. There are no words to describe Him. He is wonderful beyond all definition.

While on earth, I was privileged to listen to many eloquent pastors preach about Him, but not one ever did Him justice. He's everything I dreamed He would be, yet so much more. The angels adore Him. The saints here all worship Him. I stand in amazement of Him every day.

And the Father loves His Son, so intensely I could never explain it.

When one day you finally stand here beside me, gazing at Him in all His glory and splendor, you will be thankful you lived your life to please Him. But don't wait until you get here to crown Him Lord of all. Make Him Lord of your home and your life right now.

Remember what we read in the Bible about the apostle Peter? When he said to Jesus, "You are the Christ, the Son of the living God," Jesus replied, "You are Peter, and on this rock I will build My church."

Well, Peter (we call him the Rock Man around here) told me some really interesting things about that conversation. When Jesus said, "You are Peter," he used the Greek word *petros,* which literally means, "a small stone." But when he said, "on this rock," the word he used was *petra,* which means "a massive boulder." (Peter says Jesus was always using puns like that, especially with people's names. Too bad the English translations couldn't pick up on all those subtleties!)

The point is, Christ built His church on a firm foundation of solid rock-the proclamation that Jesus is the Son of the living God.

Now, some folks I met on earth thought Jesus was referring to Peter himself as the "rock" on which He would build His church. But Peter denies that. (Then again, he gets a lot of good-natured ribbing about anything he "denies!" He still can't believe he told people he didn't know Jesus the night that cock crowed three times. And he's detested roosters ever since!)

Peter knows first-hand about the importance of foundations. He says that, before he met Christ, his life was built on sinking sand. Every day centered around fishing, earning a living, just getting by. But the day he left the nets to follow Christ, his life changed. From that moment on, he built his life on the solid Rock.

After the Resurrection, Peter felt terrible about denying Jesus in the temple courtyard. But unlike Judas, who hanged himself under the heavy weight of guilt for what he'd done, Peter chose to confess his sins and be forgiven. That step, confession and forgiveness, allowed a simple Galilean fisherman to spend thirty years in ministry and write two of the most powerful apostolic letters in the Bible. Luke tells me the impact of those letters on the religious leaders of the day was quite impressive.

Whatever Jesus asks of you, make sure your answer is a

resounding "Yes, Lord!" If you build your life on the foundation of the Mighty One, I promise you, when the storms of life come, you will stand firm and unmoved.

I love you, Son.

Dad

Chapter 13

What Would Dad Say About Mental Health?

> All improper behavior starts with an undisciplined thought.

Dear Son,

If there is anything on earth you should protect, it is your mind.

Satan is clever at putting people into mental bondage. Some of the tools he uses to trap people are obsessions, addictions, and depression. People expend huge amounts of mental energy on these traps by focusing on them, surrendering to them, worrying about them, or trying to get over them.

While obsessions, addictions, and depressions are bad enough in themselves, the real tragedy is the time a person in bondage spends on these pointless activities. Many people up here look back on their lives and realize how much time they wasted--time that could have been spent with family or friends, in church, worship, or self-edification.

While falling into one of these mental traps may seem

like a lonely bondage, it is not. They also affect a person's family, friends, coworkers, and employers.

With the wisdom and clarity bestowed on me when I arrived here, I now understand that there is indeed a genetic basis for some people to fall into mental bondage. But there's frequently a way to avoid it. If you make an effort to understand the traps, you'll be able to save yourself and your family great agony.

One of the best things you can do to stay mentally healthy is to avoid being self-centered. Many people become absorbed in their own little world, captivated by what they're going through and how they are feeling. Though they may not realize it, they completely ignore those around them.

Self-centeredness is fertile ground for obsessions and addictions because self-centered people strive to please only themselves. This attitude leads to behaviors that can take control.

You have heard the phrase, "You are what you think." It's true. Every thought has a consequence. All improper behavior starts with an undisciplined thought. That thought, if not brought into captivity, leads to a feeling. That feeling, when fed by continual attention, leads to an action. If you do not control what you think about, you will be unable to control your behavior.

Your mind is not an amusement park to be abused with improper thoughts. Jesus said that thinking about sin is as bad as committing it.

Try to have a positive outlook on life. Even when things aren't going your way, be optimistic. Make sure all of your self-talk is positive. Encourage yourself. Everyone up here is an optimist because we know how it all ends. We win!

Be thankful all year round, not just at Thanksgiving. It's easy to focus on the things you wish were different, but don't lose sight of all the blessings you've been given.

Most people have no idea how good they have it. Look at how people have lived for most of the world's history. Folks today live significantly better than their ancestors.

Most of the people in heaven have been here for several centuries. They're absolutely astonished by the technological achievements you folks on earth have seen in recent years. Moses, for example, led hundreds of thousands of Israelites through the desert for forty years. "If I'd had GPS back then," he says, "we could have made it to the Promised Land in no time!"

Paul is amazed at how easily letters can be written and revised with today's word processors. I can't tell you how many times I've heard him say, "Why, if we'd had E-mail in my day ... "

He and the other apostles had to walk from city to city to deliver letters to the believers in Galatia, Ephesus, Philippi, Colossae, Rome. When cars were invented, Paul literally did cartwheels right out there on the streets of gold! "Imagine how quickly the believers can get the Word out now," he hollered to everyone he saw.

John the Baptist was thrilled when high-tech sound and video systems were invented. His voice, crying in the wilderness, could have reached far more people with such devices as television and radio, newspapers and magazines.

The early Bible scribes and translators shouted Hallelujah when printing presses and copy machines came out.

Yet, more often than not, people on earth can be heard

complaining about these great advancements! They angrily hang up on telemarketers when they should be happy to have a telephone at all. They are irritated when their cars or computers aren't working properly, when the copier gets jammed, their cable system doesn't get enough channels, or their satellite devices can't find the nearest McDonald's.

People complain about filth and profanity and violence in the media. Sure, Satan has infiltrated TV and movies, just like he has infected everything else God created. But rather than decry the destruction, why not rejoice in the ways these inventions can be, and are being, used for God's glory?

It isn't hard to be thankful. Get into the habit of thinking about all the good things in your life. The more you focus on your blessings, the more thankful you will be. And it's hard to become depressed if you stay grateful for the positive things in your life.

Be careful not to adopt a victim mentality. Many people take on this mind-set and become reactive in their life. You're responsible for your well-being, so be proactive in taking charge of your life. Focus on the things you can control, and leave the rest to God.

When things don't seem to be going well, accept responsibility where it is appropriate. But don't shoulder the blame for everything bad that happens.

Allow yourself to fail. Failure is not bad. Many times, it is a wonderful learning experience that can make you a better person. Earthly failure often has eternal benefits, even though people usually can't see it at the time.

You may not realize it, but I was watching when you lost that important account last week because you got stuck in traffic. I saw how upset you got, thinking you had really blown a great business deal. What you didn't know is that God allowed you to be stuck in traffic that day. Not only did you avoid a tragic car accident that would have occurred if you'd been on time, but that business deal you lost was going to end up being a terribly costly mistake, both for you and the company you were trying to strike a deal with.

I know you've had some personal failures, too. Remember that night a couple of months ago when you worked overtime, came home late and tired, and forgot about helping your daughter with her homework? Yes, I watched my granddaughter struggle with that test ... and fail anyway. I know you felt terrible about not being there for your little girl, and she felt awful about failing the test. But what I saw, and what Jesus saw, too, was that both of you learned some important lessons in that failure. And that's what God really cares about.

Learn to accept yourself as the wonderful creature God created. Here in heaven, God's plans are obvious. And believe me, He has a plan for everyone. He created each person unique for a reason. God Himself, the Creator of the universe, made you, and He is happy with His creation.

At the same time, it is important to be realistic. Don't take bits and pieces of the world around you and extrapolate them into an unrealistic perception. Don't let your mind run away with itself to the point that you get wrapped up in mental scenarios that are simply not true.

Consider the media, music, and other elements you put into your brain. Music, particularly, can have a powerful effect. There's no faster way to impact your brain. The style of music is not important, but the content carries great consequence. Be sure your music glorifies God.

I have talked a lot about how to protect your mind from those things that should not be granted entrance. But it is equally important to allow good things to be planted in your mind. The best way to do that is to focus on God's Word.

Read the Bible over and over. You don't have to read a version that's hundreds of years old to receive the truth of God's Word. Remember, versions of the Bible that are ancient today were contemporary at one time. God wants you to find a Bible you'll read, and read a lot.

The best roadmap for mental health is found in Matthew chapters five through seven, Jesus' Sermon on the Mouth. Read it, study, memorize it, and live it.

When you get here, you'll receive a new body and a renewed mind. But taking care of your mind on earth will add much to your well-being while you're still there.

I love you, Son.

Dad

Chapter 14

What Would Dad Say About Tough Times?

> God allows tough times to see how you
> will react to and deal with them.

Dear Son,

Some of the things I have shared with you so far may have been difficult to understand, but this subject might be the toughest one yet. The basis of what I have to tell you is significantly different from the understanding of almost everyone on earth.

Most people see tough times in one of three ways. They view difficult days, months, or years as:

- punishment for something they did wrong,
- unfair treatment, or
- bad luck.

I have to admit, there were times in my life, especially when I was sick and near the end of my time on earth, that I entertained some of these thoughts myself. But if you look at life through those lenses, you just open yourself up to even more pain.

I realize now why people are so inclined to these perspectives. When folks are struggling, they tend to be self-centered, totally absorbed in themselves and what is going on in their lives.

I know you've seen cases where resentment destroyed someone's life. Remember that old woman who lived down the street from us? She was a mean, cantankerous lady who never had a kind word for anyone. Well, I found out she had some really tough times in her life. And instead of letting those things direct her to God, she allowed her focus to turn inward. Her heart grew black· as it progressed from heartache to anger to bitterness.

Please don't ever let that happen to you. It's up to you to choose how you will view the tough times in your life.

Everyone goes through difficult periods. Suffering is universal, and it can be traced all the way back to original sin. (By the way, Adam and Eve are still amazed at the far-reaching consequences of that one bad choice they made to take a little bite of fruit!)

It is almost impossible to tell what someone is going through based on his or her outward appearance. That's another reason to show grace. Many people who seem to be fine outwardly are really suffering inside.

You know that newlywed couple who just joined the church? The ones who look so in love with each other they hardly notice anyone else. They really seem to have it all- a happy, romantic marriage, two brand-new cars, and a beautiful home on the hill. Well, their life isn't as perfect as it seems.

You see, that young wife is expecting their first child, and tests indicate the baby has Down Syndrome. The husband is trying to convince her to have an abortion. She doesn't want to, but he has threatened to divorce her if she refuses. So much for the image of the happy couple.

Never judge people by appearances. Almost everyone you meet will have some kind of problem. And even if it doesn't seem that big to you, it probably looks huge to them. Offer a helping hand and a listening ear every chance you get.

You cannot choose what kind of difficult times you will encounter. However, you do have two important choices to make: what perspective you will employ in dealing with the situation, and what your reaction to that situation will be.

To help you choose both your perspective and your reaction, it is important to view tough times as God does. In a discussion I had the other day with my Eternal Dad, He explained that He sees trials as *opportunities* for His children to do four things:

- Learn and Develop. Think about it. Do you grow more as a person when you're going through great times of blessing or when life is rough? In many cases, you can end tough times just by learning the lessons God is trying to teach you. When things get difficult, ask yourself, "What am I supposed to learn from this, and how does God want me to act?" Some lessons take time to sink in. But believe me, there is always a lesson to be learned.

- Glorify God. This may be hard to understand.

However, now that I am in heaven, I fully appreciate this perspective. God allows tough times to see how you will react to and deal with them.

One of the first people I went out of my way to meet after I arrived here was Job. He's a perfect example of the importance of giving God glory in the tough times. In earthly terms, he did not deserve his trials. But he used them to glorify God. The most important thing you can do is praise God in all aspects of your life—especially during the tough times.

- Draw closer to Him. We were created by God to provide Him with fellowship. Think about the good and bad times of your life. Do you normally yearn for a closer relationship with God during the good times or the bad times?

- Preparation. Once you've gone through difficulties, you will be better equipped to help others go through similar trials. Remembering how you felt and what you learned will enable you to empathize with others, not just sympathize with them.

So, when the tough times come--and they will--try to learn what you can from the experience, both for your own sake and for the benefit of others you can help. Use those times as an opportunity to draw yourself closer to God. And most importantly, be sure that God is glorified in everything.

    I love you, Son.

Dad

Chapter 15

What Would Dad Say About Faith?

> I have not heard one person say he
> trusted God too much.

Dear Son,

I've met countless people up here since I arrived. Many of them realize now that they trusted God too little during their time on earth. Yet I have not heard one person say he trusted God too much. Not one.

Obviously, everyone here has placed his faith in Christ Jesus, for it is only by grace through faith that anyone can be saved. And yes, there are some veritable giants of the faith here. Since my arrival, I have had the opportunity to meet Noah, Abraham, and David. Think for a moment about their faith.

Noah built a monstrosity of a boat, miles from the nearest body of water. He preached for 120 years, telling people God was going to send judgment on them in the form of a mighty flood. Noah says the really amazing part is that, up to that time, it had never rained anywhere on earth! Yet Noah believed God and preached away. He had faith!

Then there's Abraham, "God's friend." One day, God

told Abraham to leave his home and go to a new land, which would be revealed to him after he left. So Abraham went home to Sarah and said, "Pack your bags, honey, we're moving."

Sarah asked, "Where?"

Abraham replied, "I have no idea. I'll tell you when we get there. All I know is, God said go, so we need to go!"

If you tried something like that today, people would think you were crazy! Sarah told me she thought Abraham was absolutely out of his mind. But his faith was so strong, it was contagious. She packed her bags and left her home and followed him and God.

Now, think of David for a moment. It took more than courage for him to face that giant, Goliath. It took faith. Like Noah and Abraham before him, David believed God, against all odds.

That's what faith is all about--believing God. It's taking Him at His word, trusting Him no matter what anyone says and no matter what the circumstances.

Remember that trip we took to the Hall of Fame? Well, we have something like that up here too. But this one's different. We call it the Hall of Faith. People are not admitted to the Hall of Faith based on how many home runs they can hit or touchdown passes they can throw. Here you are admitted on the basis of your faith in God.

There are few things in life that please God more than His children believing Him, with a simple, childlike faith. God wants you to trust Him, moment by moment and day by day.

When circumstances sour, He wants you to trust Him.

When your kids struggle and stray, He wants you to trust Him. When your money runs out and the bills are staring you in the face, He wants you to trust Him. When your friends turn on you and desert you, He wants you to trust Him. Even when your health begins to slide, as mine did, or when you realize your time on earth is drawing to an end, He wants you to have faith in Him and His plans.

As I think back to my final few weeks on earth, I remember being extremely uncomfortable. During the night, I wished for day, and during the day, I wished for night. I was too weak to stand, too sick to sit, and too sore to lie in bed. I longed to die, yet at the same time, death was the last thing I wanted.

When it finally dawned on me that God was not going to answer our prayers for my physical healing, and that His appointed time for me to leave was quickly approaching, I got really scared.

As I look back on that time now, it seems silly that I allowed doubts to enter my mind. Like Peter, I took my eyes off the Master and focused on the raging waves.

I knew heaven was my eternal home. I just didn't want to go there yet. The thought of leaving your mother and you boys was unbearable for me. My faith wavered. I was unable to see what God was doing and why. But now I understand God's plan, and I praise Him for bringing me home when He did.

When God allows difficult circumstances to enter your life, He always has a reason. Learn to trust Him. He is far too holy to ever make a mistake. He is far too strong to be overcome by anyone or anything. And He is far too loving to not care about you when you're hurting.

So when the dark days come, don't blame God--bless Him. Don't curse Him--praise Him. Don't get angry with Him--run to Him with complete confidence, trusting that your Father knows best.

Do not waste your life living in fear and unbelief. Step out from the masses and determine that sink or swim, live or die, you're going to trust Him. If you focus on the rough seas, it will only be a matter of time before you sink.

Look at Him in faith. Stand firm. If you do, who knows? Perhaps you'll have a shot at heaven's Hall of Faith!

I love you, Son.

Dad

Chapter 16

What Would Dad Say About Time?

> Create a mission statement for your family,
> and make sure everything you do is
> consistent with that statement.

Dear Son,

When I arrived here in heaven, I immediately realized just how precious and short my time on earth was.

When I was a child, life seemed to move much too slowly. I spent my days wishing I was older.

When I got a little older, I lived for summer. The school year seemed to last *forever!* Then, when summer finally arrived, those three months went by so slowly I found myself actually looking forward to school again.

As an adult, I couldn't wait for the weekends, so I could take a break from work for a couple of days. And it seemed like I spent all year planning for those two short weeks of vacation.

I spent my whole life wishing time would hurry up. Then, much too soon, I realized my time on earth was running out. There were so many things I hadn't gotten around to doing, so much I'd wanted to accomplish and would never be able to.

You know, almost every single person I've met up here has told me they felt exactly the same way.

So the best suggestion I can give you related to time is to *make the best of it.* Don't waste a single moment.

Funny thing is, time is the easiest asset to waste. If you're not careful, you can throw away several years of your life without even realizing it. And once it's gone, it's gone forever. You cannot ever get back the opportunities you lose to wasted time.

The best use of your time is to invest it in things that are really important. When evaluating something you're doing, ask yourself two questions:
1. Does it make any difference in light of eternity?
2. Does it glorify God?

If you answer no to either of those questions, that activity is simply not worthy of your time.

Here are some of the things that *are* worth spending your time on:
- God. You were created to worship God. Any time you spend in worship is well invested. Drawing closer to God pleases Him, and you make yourself a better person in the process. There is no better way to enrich your life than by cultivating a close rela-tionship with God.
- Family. No one has ever arrived here wishing they'd spent a little more time working or watching television or playing golf. (Not even Payne Stewart, whom I had the distinct pleasure of meeting recently!) But most folks here do wish they'd spent

more time with their families.
- People. Invest in friendships that are mutually rewarding. Take an interest in others, even if they are not your friends. Love those who hate you. Help those who need your help. Treat others as you would want them to treat you if you were in their situation.
- Church. Serve the church God has given you. Ask yourself frequently if you are getting more out of your church than you are putting in. If so, change the scales a bit.
- Yourself. Continually make yourself a better and more valuable person. Read, study, and learn as much as you can. And don't ignore the best source of learning on earth-the Bible!

One of the best uses of your time is to establish goals for yourself and your family. Create a mission statement for your family, and make sure everything you do is consistent with that statement.

Now, I don't want to leave you with the impression that it's wrong to rest and have fun. In fact, rest is part of God's plan for you. That's a big part of what the Sabbath is all about. And God wants you to fellowship with friends, pursue hobbies, and enjoy fun activities. However, when you become consumed with pleasure, you miss the point of life, and you waste your precious time on earth.

Son, there are folks here whose lives on earth lasted only a few years. Others, just weeks or months. Many souls here never even survived to birth! All the miscarriages and abortions on earth have resulted in living souls up here who never had a single moment of earthly life. (As a matter of fact, a lot of folks are going to be surprised when they get here to realize they have brothers and sisters they have never even met.)

Then there's old Methuselah. Funny guy. He keeps us all laughing with his "what it's like to live almost a millennium" jokes--1 can't wait for you to hear them. But even he says his life on earth was brief. Compared to eternity, he's right!

Remember, life is short. So make the best of it.

I love you, Son.

Dad

Chapter 17

What Would Dad Say About Money?

> There is no correlation between financial
> success and inner happiness.

Dear Son,

What a trap money can be! Many people think it buys happiness, but that's not true. Money may allow you to do more things. But some of the most miserable people in the world are the wealthiest.

The love of money is a trick of the devil. It turns intelligent people into slaves as they chase the self-imposed bondage of the dollar.

People buy things thinking their purchases will be the missing links to their happiness. Actually, the things they buy usually only add to their misery. Sooner or later, they realize that the "high" they get from spending money is temporary and fleeting.

Many people base their self-worth on the accumulation of dollars. They seem to feel good about themselves only if they are enjoying some type of financial success. The truth is, there is no correlation between financial success and inner happiness. A person's value is not in any way tied to his financial status. The most influential man who ever lived, Jesus, was worth nothing in terms of money.

Wealth brings acquaintances, but not friends. Those who befriend wealthy people are fickle, and all-too-eager to leave when the financial advantages run dry.

After taking an informal poll of several of the residents here, I've come up with a list of suggestions for how to handle your money.

Put God First

Give to your Father God ... even before you give to your Uncle Sam.

How much should you give? Well, believers have practiced tithing all the way back to Abraham. A *tithe* means, literally, a tenth--specifically, the first tenth. But you should see that as a "floor" rather than a "ceiling." A tenth is only meant to be a starting point. The New Testament Christians did much better than a tenth. Some gave all they had.

When you tithe, you are acknowledging that God is the owner of all you possess. Therefore, honor Him with the first part of what you have rather than the leftovers.

Help Others

Many people are so afraid of someone taking advantage of them, they help no one. Be kind to those less fortunate than you. Treat them the same way you would want to be treated if you were in their situation. Teach your children, by your example, how to show compassion to the poor.

You've heard missionaries talk about conditions in places like India, Nicaragua, and the Philippines. You have seen for yourself the inner cities of Atlanta, Houston, Miami, Chicago, and New York. Rather than condemning these people for their poor choices and laziness, why not offer some grace?

Up here, Mother Teresa is much better known than all the world's billionaires put together. The reason? She cared for and gave to the poor.

Just the other day, Jesus and I were talking about the short-term missions trip you took to Cuba last year. Remember that young man you met who makes less than $20 a month? You told him you'd bring some disposable diapers and children's aspirin on your next trip. Then you gave him some cash so he could feed his little ones. You saw the expression on his face--Jesus saw the gratitude in his heart. Do you know, that man talks about your generosity to everyone he meets. And he gives all the glory to God, thanking Him for abundantly providing through you. His daughter survived a bout with pneumonia and his son accepted Christ, thanks to your gifts. They will never forget what you did--and neither will God.

Be Honest

A small discrepancy may not amount to much, but you will have to live with it. You know when you do something wrong, even if others never find out.

Someone else's mistake in your favor is no blessing. Make it right. It is better to live with a clear conscience than with all the money in the world.

Be Accountable

Find someone you completely trust to hold you accountable on financial matters. This will be a powerful tool to keep you on track.

Sacrifice Now for Security Later

Like time, after you spend your money, it's gone forever. Don't sacrifice the long term on the altar of the immediate.

Teach Your Children Financial Responsibility

This is one of the greatest blessings you can give them. Money enslaves more people than anything else. I don't want to see my grandkids become slaves to anything. Teach them to use their money wisely and to be generous.

Now, for a few things we came up with here that you *shouldn't* do with your money.

Spend More than You Take In

It's been my observation that the person who makes $30,000 a year tends to spend $32,000, while the one who makes $100,000 spends $105,000. The most fundamental rule of financial security is to spend less than you make, not more. If people followed this rule, their financial problems would disappear.

Most everyone in the U.S. is wealthy by overall world standards. It is in the areas of "comparison" and "fear of loss" that people get into trouble. The billionaire who loses a lot of money and only has a few million left feels just as bad as the poor man who loses his last dime.

The problem is focus. People are often so worried about losing what they have that they throw away what is really important. In their vain search for financial freedom, they end up in financial bondage.

Borrow

Avoid the popular "live for today" mentality. Spend within your means.

Be Gullible

If a financial deal seems too good to be true, it probably is. Don't fall for long shots like the lottery, gambling, or other "get rich quick" schemes.

John Wesley told me to remind you of a saying he came up with while on earth. "Make all you can, save all you can, and most importantly, give all you can." Now, that's sound financial advice!

What Jesus said 2000 years ago is still true. Where your treasure is, there will your heart be also.

I love you, Son.

Dad

Chapter 18

What Would Dad Say About Science?

> Earthly science is man's mortal attempt to
> understand the world God created.

Dear Son,

One of the first things I realized after arriving here in heaven was how little I really understood about how the world works. I am amazed at how much I learned once my mind was set free of all the incorrect theories and incomplete paradigms I had accepted as truth on earth.

To begin with, I learned that the Bible really is true! All of it! Even Christians can sometimes doubt God's Word. But have faith. You, too, will understand how true it all is when you get here.

Some scientists on earth like to talk about how much they know. But even they admit that science is constantly coming up with new theories that disprove highly regarded and accepted "truths." Much of what is accepted as fact today is ludicrous when viewed through the eyes of perfect knowledge. Even the most self-assured scientists admit that there is much they don't yet understand. In fact, those who are honest will admit that what they *don't* comprehend is far greater than what they do.

Up here, I have met many of the world's most brilliant scientists. When their eyes were opened, they recognized how little they really knew in their earthly wisdom. Once they received the full knowledge of His master plan for the world, they felt pretty foolish for ever having doubted Him.

I want to share with you a funny thing that happened to me recently. The other day, while you were sleeping, I went to a meeting of some of the most brilliant scientists who ever lived. They like to get together frequently and discuss their amazement at God's wonderful plan for creating and sustaining the world. They were praising and glorifying God for His wonderful work and marveling at the ingenuity of it all.

Isaac Newton and Albert Einstein were there, among many other renowned scientists. (Yes, I was surprised to see Einstein here, too. But he told me a Christian in New Jersey shared the gospel with him shortly before he died. Praise the Lord!)

The funny part of this meeting for me was hearing these scientists laughing at themselves. In their new state of perfect knowledge, they find it hilarious to think about how brilliant they thought they were on earth. They're tickled to realize how little they understood while they were living in the world they thought they knew so much about.

Earthly science is man's mortal attempt to understand the world God created. By taking the Lord out of the equation, no solution--however well thought out, tested, or rational it may be--will be accurate.

God has not yet revealed everything to those still living in the world. I wish I could share with you some of the vast knowledge I have gleaned here. But it is not in God's plan for those on earth to fully understand His ways. He much prefers His people to take Him on faith.

Many scientific theories require significantly more faith than it takes to trust God's Word. Probably the best example of this is evolution. Believing that all the beautiful and intricate aspects of nature--from flowers and trees, to birds and animals and insects, to human beings--"just happened," with no plan or power to create them ... that takes significantly more faith than simply accepting that God designed and created the world and everything in it. From the perspective of heaven, it seems obvious, and it will be made clear to everyone on earth, sooner or later.

But let me offer a word of caution here. You shouldn't look down on those unenlightened people who don't accept the truth. They don't understand because they have been deceived by the very enemy of truth, Satan himself.

Do you remember the seminar that local church conducted on Evolution vs. Creationism? It was advertised as an objective look at both sides by authorities in scientific fields. The pews were packed that day, with both Christians and unbelievers. We were all praising God up here for the evangelistic opportunities this seminar represented.

Unfortunately, the moderator addressed his comments exclusively to Christians, claiming that this panel of experts could help believers "show those deluded idiots who fall for the inane rantings of Darwinism how stupid. and wrong they are."

There was silence here in heaven at that moment as we watched skeptical hearts grow harder and colder toward Christianity. No amount of empirical evidence could overcome the spirit of judgment and condemnation that moderator created.

So when you come across people who put their faith in science rather than the Lord, don't put them down--love them. Learn why they believe what they do so you can communicate with them intelligently and gently lead them a little closer to the truth.

Above all, I encourage you to keep your faith in the inerrancy of God's Word until the day when you, too, have perfect knowledge. Trust me, you'll be glad you did.

I love you, Son.

Dad

Chapter 19

What Would Dad Say About Church Traditions?

> Emphasize what's important.
> Don't quibble over what's not.

Dear Son,

I took a lot of things very seriously during my life on earth. I realize now that some of those issues really were important, but others were not.

One area I placed far too much importance on was church traditions. I see now that my adherence to "traditionalism" sometimes caused me to alienate myself from the very world Christ died for--the world I was commissioned to reach.

Now, don't get me wrong. Many church traditions are beautiful and should be treasured. When used properly, they become valuable tools that assist in the worship and service of God. But if you're not careful, traditions can become 111ore important to you than God. Sometimes, they create a wall that separates you from Him and isolates you from a lost and hurting world desperately in need of a Savior.

When traditions become walls, you need to tear them

down. Remember, Jesus reserved His most harsh criticism for the Pharisees who were bound by, and in bondage to, their traditions.

Let me give you some examples.

Attire

Believe it or not, up here it doesn't matter if you wear a coat and tie when you preach! I've been walking around this place for years now, and I have yet to see Jesus wear a suit.

Schedules

We don't start services at 11:00 sharp and end at 12:00 dull. Worship here last for days at a time. In fact, this place is really one ongoing, perpetual time of worship. Our praises of Him never cease!

Segregation

The diversity of heaven is stunning, to say the least! We have folks here from every corner of the globe. People of every race, color, and language worship together as one. You've never heard worship like we have here! And you ought to see the look on our Lord's face as we worship Him together in peace and harmony. He is so pleased!

Music

The music here is absolutely heavenly! Sometimes we skip a verse or two of a song, and other times we sing the same song a dozen times. Yet all too often, good Christian people on earth argue heatedly over what kind of music to sing in their church services. Some demand traditional hymns, while others insist the music be jazzed up. I've seen people actually stand in judgment of others and ridicule them in public simply because of their preferences in music. Unbelievable!

Guess what? Up here, we have all types of music--most of which no one on earth has even heard. I'll admit, at first it felt strange to worship God using different kinds of music. But the way we look at it, God is far too awesome to be praised with just one style. Here, all music blends together into one magnificent doxology of praise.

Style

Worship here is a precious time filled with variety. Sometimes we stand quietly in awe of Him. Occasionally, we bow on our faces at His feet. Often, we sing and shout our hallelujahs. At other times, we close our mouths and silently adore Him. You see, worship is not about style. It's about directing our attention to Him. When we do, everything else pales into insignificance.

There's a simple solution to all these disagreements. Emphasize what's important. Don't quibble over what's not. I realize now how silly most church fights are. God is dishonored by the lack of unity in some of His churches today. From our vantage point, all the fussing and fighting over traditions and preferences seems downright childish.

The very meaning of the word *worship* carries with it the idea of bowing down before Him, being overwhelmed by the awesome glory of His presence, and humbly praising and thanking Him for all He is and all He has done. That's what He deserves, and that's what He desires. Give it to Him!

See yourself as a missionary to a society that, for the most part, has not grown up in a Bible-centered home, as you did, and does not know God as their Father. Most of those with whom you come into contact know one thing about the church: It's full of hypocrites! Challenge their perception of our Lord's church by graciously accepting them and treating them with love.

When people show up at your church dressed differently from everyone else, don't allow your preferences to drive them away. Reach out to them. Don't condemn them---care for them. Look at them through the eyes of our Savior. Learn to be separated from sin without becoming isolated from sinners. Love them into the arms of Jesus!

You may not see it, but every day, you are surrounded by people who have been hurt in the church or mistreated and judged by people claiming to be Christians. Many of these folks think Christians despise them. Prove them wrong!

You shouldn't live out of touch with your culture. Christ told you to be the light of the world, not the light of the church. Don't hide in your worship center, preaching only to the deacons and the choir. Do not shun the tongue-studded teen, or the gang kid with baggy pants, or even the black- caped Satanist. You needn't be afraid that they'll somehow infect you. Look beyond their pierced bodies and see their broken hearts.

So keep your church traditions, and enjoy them. But remember, the ultimate goal is to do all things in a manner that honors and pleases your Lord.

I love you, Son.

Dad

Chapter 20

What Would Dad Say About Life?

> You have a very short time in which to
> make an impact on the world.

Dear Son,

Probably the most important thing I can tell you about life is that you only get one chance. And that one chance goes by fast! It is but a blink of your eye in the framework of eternity.

I know, with your earthly mind, it is difficult to comprehend the concept of your lifespan as compared to forever. So let me give you three examples that may help you understand. The entire length of your life, when compared to eternity, is like:

- a single drop of water out of all the world's oceans
- a speck of sand out of all the world's beaches and deserts combined
- one inch of all the world's roads and highways put together.

Actually, even those examples don't begin to scratch the surface.

My point is not to downplay the significance of your

life, but to stress its importance. You have a very short time in which to make an impact on the world. Don't waste it.

Many people place a higher priority on the pursuit of happiness than on the really important aspects of life. Interestingly, while the pursuit of happiness may bring momentary pleasure, it does not result in true joy. The search for happiness is a never-ending treadmill. It is a thirst that cannot be quenched. And that is real bondage!

True happiness comes from putting God, your family, and other people first. Funny thing is, when you put others first, God always blesses you more abundantly.

When you do good deeds in secret, you touch God's heart, and you will receive eternal rewards for your earthly actions. But if you run after compliments by letting people know about the things you have done, your reward stops there. It is the only praise you will receive.

Let me give you an analogy that you may find helpful. What would you do if I told you that, if you did sit-ups for the next thirty seconds, you would live the next forty years of your life in absolute luxury as the richest man on earth? I don't even need to ask, because I know what you would do. You would be down on the floor doing sit-ups! And, knowing you as I do, you would probably do them for thirty *minutes,* just in case. You would be willing to make the minuscule investment necessary to obtain the years of riches.

That analogy does not even begin to do justice to what your time on earth is like compared to eternity. Every little thing you do for God on earth will have eternal effects and will bring you more abundant joy than you could possibly imagine.

You will be in heaven with me before you know it. In the blink of an eye, the temporary life you now live will give way to an eternity of living beyond your wildest dreams. I know, because that's what happened to me!

When you have fulfilled, in your earthly life, all the things God has for you to do, He will bring you here. This is where your real life will truly begin.

The first person God will introduce you to is His beloved, begotten Son, Jesus. I know how much you are looking forward to that!

After you have spent some time with your Savior, I will be first in line to greet you. We will enjoy a great big bear hug, for as long as we want.

Then I will start introducing you to the people I've met up here. I can't tell you how exciting it is to sit down and talk face to face with Old Testament heroes like Adam, Abraham, Isaac, Jacob, Moses, Joshua, David, and all the "major" and "minor" prophets. Just wait till you hear the story of Balaam and his talking donkey straight from the horse's mouth, so to speak!

I've loved getting to know personally the men of the New Testament who walked with Jesus on earth and were the first to spread the gospel. John the Baptist, Joseph, Lazarus, Paul, and the disciples are all truly fascinating people!

The women of the Bible also have wonderful stories to tell, many of which were not recorded in much detail in the Scriptures. I've loved listening to Eve, Ruth, Esther, Bathsheba, Rahab, the "excellent wife" of Proverbs 31, Martha and Mary, the woman at the well, Mary Magdalene, Jairus's daughter, and Jesus' mother Mary.

The Bible says that Jesus did many things beyond what was written about in the New Testament. Fortunately, we have all eternity to hear the stories. And I never get tired of listening to them.

And just wait until you meet people like C. S. Lewis, Joan of Arc, Dwight L. Moody, Mother Teresa, and all those other folks you've read and heard so much about. They are surprisingly humble people, considering all they accomplished on earth for God's kingdom.

It is fascinating to hear the accounts of every person here, how God reached into their lives in a personal way to touch their hearts and bring them into the family of God. When you arrive, you will be amazed to see some people here you would never have thought could make it to heaven. God's grace is more far-reaching than you could ever imagine!

Your heart will burst with joy as you meet the many people who made it to heaven because of something you said or did on earth. You have no idea how much impact your words and deeds have had for eternity. And the effect is truly exponential. For every single person you brought closer to God's kingdom, all the people that person reached for Christ will want to thank you too. And all the people those folks witnessed to ... Well, you get the picture!

All of your relatives who have gotten here before you are eager to see you as well. You have cousins and aunts and uncles and grandparents back countless generations who prayed for you during their lives on earth, and continue to pray for you from their perfect vantage point of heaven.

There's one more person here who is very excited to

meet you. Remember when your wife had that miscarriage? It happened so early in her pregnancy, very few people even knew about it. But God did. It's true--life begins at conception, not birth. From the moment that child was conceived, she had a soul. Yes, Son, you have a daughter you've never met, and that little girl can hardly wait to say hi to her earthly daddy for the first time.

So live your life well. Make us all proud. Please God in everything you do. You'll be glad you did!

And always remember, I'll be waiting for you at the Eastern Gate.

I love you, Son.

Dad

Conclusion

Dear Reader,

As Bill and I have written this book, the concept that repeatedly impressed itself upon me was that much, if not most, of what we do on earth is of little importance. Bluntly put, the majority of what we concern ourselves with does not matter at all in light of eternity.

Time and again the following Scripture has passed through my mind: "Since then you have been raised with Christ, set your beans on things above, where Christ is seated at the right hand of God. Set your minds on things above, not on earthly things." (Colossians 3:1-2 NIV)

Someone has suggested that the only certainty in life is death. Death is definitely a sure thing, but so is life after death. There is a God. There is a heaven. And yes, there is a hell. We will all die. We will face our Creator, God. This is a certainty. In light of this reality, it becomes imperative for us to live our lives with eternity in view.

To do so means investing ourselves in those things that have eternal value. It means making people a priority over things. People are eternal - possessions are not. The newest car in the neighborhood will one day be an old clunker. The most impressive house on the block will someday lie in disrepair. The most expensive clothing will one day be ragged and out of style. The name brand you purchase today will be hauled off to Goodwill tomorrow.

An old Chinese proverb says, "If you want a one-year harvest, plant wheat. If you want a ten-year harvest, plant trees. If you want a lifetime harvest, plant people." Amen!

I encourage you to do what Bill and I have done. Take inventory of your life in view of eternity. Are people truly your priority? What about those closest to you, your family? Are they first in your life? Do they know it? Are you serving those around you in love? Are you using your God-given talents to help people? Or is your life wrapped up in the material possessions you've accumulated along the way?

Invest yourself in things eternal, things that count. Spend your most precious commodity--time--on matters that really matter.

The most important thing you can do for yourself, and your family, is to decide where you will spend eternity. If you have not already done so, I encourage you to open your heart to Jesus Christ. He loves us more than anyone this side of heaven can comprehend. Jesus' death on the cross proved God's love, once and for all.

Since you will live on after death, why not choose to live in the presence of God, along with your loved ones who have also chosen heaven? Christ once asked, "What shall it profit a man if he gains the whole world and yet loses his own soul?"

Before you close this book, pause and pray to your heavenly Father. Ask Him to forgive your sins and to write your name in His eternal book of life. Take Jesus to be your personal Lord and Savior right now. Don't put off the most important decision you will ever make. You never know at what moment eternity will begin for you.

Once you've made that momentous decision, do your best to live as Jesus lived. Try to look at your life from an eternal perspective, and adjust your priorities accordingly. As you do, you will discover a life of unspeakable joy!

And when you someday pass from this earth into heaven, those who've gone before you will be awaiting your arrival. When you get to the Eastern Gate, look for my dad. He'll be expecting you. He's been watching as you've read this book. He cheered when you opened its cover. I know he's eager to meet you and talk about how this message has changed your life.

Jesus loves you.

David

About Our Dads

Bill's Dad
WILLIAM YEARGIN

William Yeargin was born on January 8, 1933, in Oxford, North Carolina, where he lived until he graduated from high school. After attending North Carolina State University, William enlisted in the U.S. Army, serving in Asia. After his military service, he moved to Florida and worked for Pratt & Whitney Aircraft until his retirement nearly thirty-five years later.

William married the love of his life, Dottie Herbert, on October 25, 1958. They remained married until William's death forty years later. William and Dottie have two children, Bill and Doug. They are the proud grandparents of six grandchildren: Erin, Amanda, Rachel, Jonathan, Joshua, and Luke.

William served as a deacon, trustee, and teacher in his church. He was the quintessential father and prayer warrior.

William began his life in heaven on July 5, 1998.

David's Dad
MACK NELMS

Mack Nelms was born on November 7, 1923, in Suffolk, Virginia. His family moved to Georgia when he was two years old. After graduating from high school, Mack enlisted in the U.S. Navy, serving as a pilot in the Naval Air Corps. Mack worked for Southern Bell from the time he left the Navy until his retirement.

Mack married his high school sweetheart, Nan Smith, on June 15, 1947. They remained married until Mack's death forty-seven years later. Mack and Nan have four children, three of whom are in the ministry. They are the proud grandparents of eleven grandchildren.

Mack served as a deacon, trustee, teacher, and Sunday school superintendent in his church. At the age of 70, he assumed the pastorate of a small country church in rural Georgia.

Mack's homecoming occurred on February 17, 1995. He left earth at the age of seventy-two doing what he loved most--serving his Lord.

www.ingramcontent.com/pod-product-compliance
Lightning Source LLC
Chambersburg PA
CBHW072037110526
44592CB00012B/1460